Contents

List of figures x
List of acronyms and abbreviations xi
Audience xiii
Acknowledgements xiv

Introduction 1
    Scope of content 1

Part I: Initiation 3

Chapter 1: Intranets explained 4
    So what is an Intranet? 4
    The technology 6
    Cross-platform compatibility 7
    Global access 7
    Ease-of-use 7
    Flexibility 7
    Open standards 7
    Cost 7
    Business benefits 8

Chapter 2: Models for Implementation 9
    Stage 1: Initiation 10

Chapter 3: Costing your Intranet 11
    Client server costs 11
    Server set-up costs 12
    Networking infrastructure 12
    Content creation 12
    Training costs 12
3.1 Calculating Returns-On-Investment (ROIs) 13
    Costs (investment) 13
    Savings (returns) 13
3.2 ROI Case study 14

Chapter 4: Outsourcing **18**

Part II: Contagion **23**

Chapter 5: Achieving Critical Mass **24**

Stage 2: Contagion 24

Chapter 6: Barriers to Access.. **25**

Access points 25
Cultural aspects 25
A case study: Xerox 26

Chapter 7: Information Supply and Retrieval **29**

Search engines...29
Intelligent agents 31
Portals 32
Portals: purchasing issues 34

Chapter 8: Filling the Intranet **36**

Flat content 36
Interactive content 37
Commercial or externally-sourced information 38
Business Intelligence information 39
8.1 Legacy systems..40
Launching legacy systems via web-based menus 41
Convert existing documentation using conversion utilities.............42

Chapter 9: Business Applications and Services **44**

9.1 The personnel department 44
9.2 Library and Information Services..45
9.3 IT department..46
9.4 Training, education and e-learning 47

Part III: Control **53**

Chapter 10: Procedures and Standardisation 54

Stage 3: Control 54

Chapter 11: Content Management Issues 55

Ownership of content 55
11.1 Management structures 59
Intranet management structures, example 1. 59
Webmaster and team 59
Local Intranet managers 59
Local Intranet developers 60
Information owners 60
Intranet management structures, example 2. 61
Intranet Management Group (IMG) 62
Content authorisers 62
Content providers 62
Editorial board 62
Service provider 63
Intranet Technical Sub-Committee 63
11.2 Electronic Document Management Systems 63
Version control 64
Storage of metadata 64
Security 65
Check-in/check-out facility 65
Search and indexing 66
File interdependencies and groupings utilities 66
Open standard interfaces 66
Structure and organisational capabilities 67
Supports multiple file types 67
Maintain file expiration dates 67
11.3 Content management and extranets 69

Chapter 12: Enhancing Web Content 72

Chapter 13: Implementing a Publishing Policy 75

Chapter 14: Information Overload 76

Email filters 79
Rerouting 'spam' 79
Unsubscribe to services and updates 80
Things to watch out for before you send 80
Training 81
Selective browsing 82

Part IV: Integration 83

Chapter 15: Integrating Knowledge Management with your Intranet Strategy 84

Stage 4: integration 84
Knowledge Management: the definition 85

Chapter 16: Groupware 87

What is Groupware? 87
16.1 Shared reference library 88
16.2 Computer-Supported Collaborative Working (CSCW) systems 88
Purchasing issues 91
16.3 Workflow management systems 91
Availability of graphic tools 93
Routing capability 93
The establishment of groups 93
Performance metrics 93
Queue management 93
Management of events 93
Workload 93
Integration capacity 93
Monitoring 94
Simulation 94
Webflow 94
Task management 94
Process management 94
Documentation 95
Hardware and software considerations 95
Human factors 95
Process analysts and designers 95
Vendor/product reputation 95

Technical support 96
Canvass user needs 96
Acceptance 96
Cost of product 96

Chapter 17: Extranets 99

17.1 Remote workers 100
17.2 Teleworking 101
Cost savings 101
Increased productivity 101
Improved motivation 101
Organisation flexibility 101
Resilience 102
Benefits for individuals 102
Disadvantages 102
17.3 Customer and supplier systems 105
Customers 105
Scalability 106
Integration 106
Functionality 107
Multichannel 107
User interface: customer 107
User interface: agent 108
Vendor viability 108
Suppliers 109

Chapter 18: Implementing an Extranet 112

18.1 Remote access 'networked services' 113
Public 113
Managed 113
Internet-based 113
Fears 114

Chapter 19: Transnational Intranets and Extranets 115

Language 115
Legal matters - encryption 118
Legal matters – EU Data Protection 118

Standardising client interfaces 119
A case study: Arthur Andersen 120

Chapter 20: Security 122

Overview of BS 7799 123
Data Protection Act and BS 7799 124
Internet/Intranet misuse 125
Internet Access Control 126
The Regulation of Investigatory Powers (RIP) Bill 128
Identifying security needs and measures 130

Part V: Pervasion 131

Chapter 21: Future Developments 132

21.1 Mobile and Wireless Computing 132
Web to mobile content 134
21.2 Application Service Providers 135
21.3 Unified Messaging 137
Improved customer satisfaction 138
A more efficient organisation 139
Reduced cost 139
21.4 Instant Messaging 140
21.5 Voice over IP 142

Chapter 22: The Everywhere-net 144

Ubiquitous Computing 144
Personal Area Networks 145
Pervasion, the fifth stage of Intranet development 146

References 150

Appendices 161

Appendix A: Sample 'Computer Network and Internet Access Policy' .. 161
Disclaimer 161
Permitted Use of Internet and Company Computer Network 161

Computer Network Use Limitations 162
Duty Not to Waste or Damage Computer Resources 162
No Expectation of Privacy 163
Acknowledgement of Understanding 163

Further Reading 165

Groupwork, Content Management and Workflow 165
Departmental Applications 166
Extranets 166
Information Overload 167
Intranet Design 167
Intranet Management 167
Miscellaneous 167
Mobile Technologies and Teleworking 168
Retrieval Technologies 168
Security (and data protection) 168
Training and Education 168
Transnational Intranets 168

Index 169

List of figures

Figure 1. A progressive model for Intranet development 9

Figure 2. Staged methodology for Intranet implementation 20

Figure 3. Converging ICT market sectors and Intranet
service providers 21

Figure 4. List of portal product and service vendors 35

Figure 5. Stages of Intranet maturity 36

Figure 6. A sample organisational structure for managing
Intranet publishing 61

Figure 7. Comparative costs for several leading Document
Management Systems 68

Figure 8. List of Internet security specialists and software vendors 129

Figure 9. A proposed 5th stage of Intranet development 147

List of acronyms and abbreviations

ASP   Application Services Provider

CRM   Customer Relationship Management

CSCL   Computer Supported Collaborative Learning

CSCW Computer Supported Collaborative Working

DMS   Document Management System

DSL   Digital Subscriber Line

EIP   Enterprise Information Protocol

ERP   Enterprise Resource Planning

ESP   Extranet Service Provider

FAQ   Frequently Asked Question(s)

FTP   File Transfer Protocol

GPRS   General Packet Radio Services

HR   Human resources

HTML HyperText Mark-up Language

HTTP   HyperText Transfer Protocol

IAC   Internet Access Control

IAM   Internet Access Management

IAP   Internet Access Provider

ICQ   "I Seek U"

ICT   Information & Communication Technology

IM   Instant Messaging

IP   Internet Protocol

IR   Information Retrieval

ISDN   Integrated Services Digital Network

ISP   Internet Service Provider

LAN   Local Area Network

LIS   Library & Information Services

MIS   Management Information Systems

ODBC   Open Database Connectivity

PAN   Personal Area Network

PDA   Personal Digital Assistant

PDF   Portable Document Format

PSTN   Public Switched Telephone Network

ROI   Return-on-investment

SMTP   Simple Mail Transfer Protocol

TCP/IP Transport Control Protocol / Internet Protocol

UM   Unified Messaging

VoIP   Voice over Internet Protocol

VPN   Virtual Private Network

WAN   Wide Area Network

WAP   Wireless Application Protocol

WFMS   WorkFlow Management Systems

WML   Wireless Mark-up Language

Audience

This book may appeal to anyone requiring an overview of the technological and cultural implications of adopting information and knowledge management solutions using Internet technologies.

The book examines the tactical issues addressed at a functional or departmental level and their impact upon the organisation as a whole from a strategic perspective. Due to the integral and pervasive nature of an Intranet throughout all areas and levels of an organisation, the content of this book may appeal to a range of employees, regardless of remit or seniority. The book is likely to be of interest to those making contributions to the infrastructure and content of an Intranet, as well as to those responsible for securing the funding and planning for the Intranet's future development.

The broad overview of information systems and enabling technologies examined may also make useful reading for undergraduates and postgraduates of educational programmes that contain curriculum content such as information management and systems, ICT project management, strategic information management and knowledge management.

Acknowledgements

I would like to thank all of the people who have helped during the research of the book who have included the publishers, friends, and associates across a wide number of professions. I am also grateful to contributors from the following organisations that have taken the time to provide valuable information and advice throughout the books compilation:

Alstom Drives & Controls Ltd
ASDA Stores PLC
BAe Systems PLC
Blackwell Publishers Ltd
Brighton Business School
British Airport Authorities PLC
BT Laboratories
Building Design Partnership
Burmah Castrol
Clearview Systems
Compaq
Cornhill Insurance PLC
Danzas Management Ltd.
Dewsbury College
ESIEA
European Commission
Fujitsu Europe Telecom R&D Centre Ltd
GlaxoWellcome R&D
IFR Ltd
Interactive Consulting Group
Lex Service PLC
Lexis-Nexus
Medical Research Council (MRC)
Merck Sharp & Dohme Research
Monsanto Inc.
Montgomery Watson
Mott MacDonald Group
National Air Traffic Services Ltd
National Grid
National Library for the Blind
Natural History Museum
Open University
Pioneer
PricewaterhouseCoopers
RAC Motoring Services
Scottish FE & HE Funding Councils
Sheffield Hallam University

Shell UK Oil Products Ltd
Siemens Business Services Ltd
Siemens Communications Ltd
Sweet & Maxwell Ltd
TA Group
Technical University of Crete
TMS Group
University of Northumbria at Newcastle
Verity, Inc.
Vodafone Corporate
Warwickshire College
West Cheshire College
Writtle College

Above all, I am indebted to my wife, Kate, who has quietly and patiently persevered over the last 18 months whilst paper-based mountains of product literature, books, post-it notes, spreadsheets, journal articles, and magazine cuttings have grown in every conceivable corner of our abode!

Introduction

Scope of content

With the advent of the World Wide Web, came its navigation tool - the 'web browser'. This quickly become recognised as the 'Swiss army knife of the Internet' due to its wide range of information retrieval capabilities and intuitive graphical user interface (GUI).

It was not long before organisations caught on to the idea that such a powerful one-stop information tool could be adapted easily by organisations for use on their networks or internal webs to improve communication, cut costs, speed up business processes and, more recently, increase revenue through e-commerce applications.

Unfortunately no one has yet come up with a generic or de facto formula for successfully implementing an Intranet across all kinds of organisations. Arguments for the most appropriate strategies for implementation are still being debated. Several factors may be contributing to this position.

From a general perspective these aspects may include:

- Changing technology
- Changing business practices
- Changing legal issues

From an organisational perspective the dominant issues may be:

- Different working cultures and values
- Different (or constantly changing) market sectors
- Different sizes and management structures
- Different success rates and histories of implementing technological solutions

Even in the short history of Intranet usage, its strategic value can be seen to have changed from being solely a communication tool to include the integration of Knowledge Management strategies. More recently it has been seen as the backbone of any e-commerce strategy. This series of radi-

cal changes in strategic focus over such a short period illustrates poign-
antly the challenge that is faced by anyone studying and/or implementing
and developing an Intranet (not to mention researching it!).

What has happened, however, is that surveys and case studies have over
the years highlighted the stages of Intranet development and their respective failures and successes. As a result, a series of models have been
developed to help other organisations map the technology and ideas onto
their organisation and plan for future developments. Hopefully this will
help to minimise the risks associated with implementing such monumen-
tal shifts in culture, business operations and technological infrastructure.

This book therefore aims to review some of the case studies, market predictions, evolving technologies and the strategic approaches that have
been adopted by organisations. The intention is to enable the reader to
form an overview of the many different aspects that are enveloped through
the design, implementation and management of Intranets and provide
the opportunity to take or apply the more relevant aspects in the context
of their own learning or working environments.

Part 1

Initiation

Chapter 1

Intranets explained

Intranets are generally considered, and on the whole justly proven, to be inexpensive to implement. However, the ensuing operational and development issues become far more complex and require a significant amount of thought, planning and nurturing than may initially be envisaged. Subsequently, costs begin to climb, especially as more interactive systems are embraced on the Intranet such as legacy and backoffice systems, along with dedicated web-based e-commerce solutions.

Intranets are now emerging from a recent history, where they were commonly regarded as a cheap and cheerful means of meeting an organisation's information dissemination needs. The realisation has now emerged that there is more to be gained from these enabling Internet technologies than merely reaping a quick Return-on-Investment (ROI) through savings on reprographics and distribution costs.

Five years on from a time when pioneering organisations first implemented corporate-wide Intranets (Aslib, 1996) and claimed massive costs savings in reprographics and publishing, these same organisations are now realising that the technology can offer greater rewards. With the advent of more sophisticated technology and applications, that greater reflect core business aims, the Intranet has become recognised as a strategic tool to nurture the identification, sharing, and creation of an organisation's intellectual and knowledge assets. In short, many large organisations now regard their Intranet as the corporate memory.

This chapter aims to discuss how this transformation can be realised and reflect upon many of the painful lessons learnt by these organisations, so that they may be re-addressed to aid the further exploitation of Internet technologies to provide greater business value.

So what is an Intranet?

Due to the fact that Intranets frequently cross organisational boundaries and 'touch' all functional areas and departments, even the process of defining an Intranet can be more complicated than first thought.

An Intranet may be seen to be different things to different people depending on the perspective held by each individual and their respective job function and department (or even their relationship to the organisation as a whole if they are a supplier or customer).

Generally, definitions will relate to:

i]   a technological viewpoint concentrating on Intranets purely from the perspective of software, hardware and networking protocols or;

ii]   an operational and process perspective concerned with the business-value that such a tool brings to the organisation

Any other definitions will generally be seen to fall somewhere in between the two. Examples of how an Intranet may be perceived by individual employees according to their respective job functions, may include the following two extremes:

…that of an IT Manager who may well define an Intranet as:

'…an IP-based network of nodes behind a firewall, or behind several firewalls connected by secure, possibly virtual, networks.'

(Intranet Design Magazine, 1999)

…whilst a member of the Senior Management Team may refer to an Intranet as:

'…an organisation's corporate memory.'

(Kuhn and Abecker, 1999)

Both of these definitions may be argued to be equally valid. Ordinarily, and from a practical perspective, establishing such a definition for a technology or business process would normally be regarded as a case of mere semantics. The important issue would typically be that each department or function using the technology should come to a common agreement on a definition that was relevant to their respective business-concerns.

However because of the pervasive nature of an effective Intranet spanning the organisation, all business functions and employees will have some involvement with its development or use. As a result, cross-functional relationships will develop that did not previously exist and standards will need to be created jointly and adhered to by departments who previously may have had no common ground with other departments, apart from being part of the same organisation.

For these new partnerships and teams to succeed in implementing and developing an Intranet it is important that each has an understanding of the different perspectives and interpretations held by different parties in terms of what they perceive the Intranet to be and what benefits it has to offer.

In trying to take into consideration as many of these differing perspectives and contexts as possible, this chapter will adopt the fairly wide definition for an Intranet as prescribed by the Institute of Management (Irving and McWilliams, 1999).

> 'An Intranet is a private, corporate network that uses Internet products and technologies. Access to an Intranet is controlled by the organisation that established it, and is often restricted just to employees. Occasionally, however, suppliers and customers can also be given access to parts of it.'

The latter proviso referring to suppliers and customers can also include remote employees in the field or at home. This form of access to an Intranet is known as an extranet and will be examined further in chapter 17.

The technology

In researching issues relating to the contents of this book, several organisations, which have implemented Intranets of substantial size or maturity, were surveyed by questionnaire with regard to the methods, technology and policies used to implement the use of Internet technologies on their respective internal networks.

In responding to one of the survey questions regarding the start-up date of his company's Intranet, one Principal Engineer replied that his company had already implemented an Intranet when he joined the company in 1987. Those with a general knowledge of Internet history and who find nothing surprising in this statement may wish to jump to the next section.

For those who may be surprised by the claim that an Intranet could exist in 1987 (several years before the advent of the World Wide Web) the following background information may be useful in understanding why Intranets have become such powerful communication and effective business tools.

An introduction to a book such as this could not avoid first briefly referring to the underlying technology that has made the development of the Intranet possible.

First off, to explain the response made by the respondent mentioned above; his reply referred to the fact that his company had been using email on the organisation's worldwide TCP/IP-based network. IP-based (Internet Protocol) networks have been around since the late 1960s and available for any individual or organisation to use as a networking platform.

TCP/IP is the Internet protocol that acts as a network carrier for other closely related protocols and services that include the World Wide Web (HTTP – HyperText Transfer Protocol), E-mail (SMTP – Simple Mail Transfer Protocol), FTP (File Transfer Protocol), Gopher (menu-driven system for document retrieval), Telnet (a remote terminal connection service), IRC (Internet Relay Chat) etc.

Although many of these services still exist, in many cases they have been replaced, subsumed or web-enabled within the web browser interface. Therefore, the so-called 'killer applications' now associated with the Internet are email (electronic mail) and the web browser (e.g. MS Internet Explorer, Netscape Navigator, etc.). It should also be acknowledged here that the vast majority of email systems also provide access via the web browser interface.

The main reasons generally cited for the web browser becoming so successful are often attributed to the following (Bernard, 1998):

Cross-platform compatibility

The World Wide Web protocol (http) is platform-independent so any individual web document on the Internet can be accessed across all platforms e.g. PC, Unix, Apple Macintosh or Linux, etc.

Global access

Documents can be requested seamlessly from any server located on any TCP/IP network like the Internet or private network such as an Intranet.

Ease-of-use

The Hypertext (or hyperlink) Transfer Protocol allows documents and multimedia to be simply retrieved without the user needing to know the specific location of a file or its name.

Flexibility

The web browser has evolved to enable seamless access to be gained to various server types (Web, gopher, SMTP, ftp, etc.) and may be configured to recognise any file types and launch the respective application to view any proprietary file formats such as MS Word, Excel, PDF etc. WWW servers can also provide access to backoffice legacy systems such as databases and in-house developed applications.

Open standards

Any software that uses the published standards can be used as a browser or HTML editor.

Cost

The only cost associated with using web browsers is related to those incurred in installing or configuring the web browser itself. Of course all of the factors above have some kind of economic benefit associated with them. However, one of the most significant cost saving first recognised by organisations who realised that web browsers could be used on private internal networks (Intranets), was that this was a sophisticated graphical user interface that would operate across any platform and was available as either freeware or inexpensive shareware.

Business benefits

Apart from the obvious cost savings in reprographics, organisations quickly observed additional benefits arising as the Intranet began to transform the way in which the organisation was communicating and refining business processes. KPMG, the global finance and management consultancy (KPMG, 1997) highlighted the main benefits of these transformations as:

- Releasing the latent value of the information it [the organisation] holds
- Sharing the use of the information
- Allowing expertise and intellectual skills to be exploited more widely
- Encouraging teams to work and grow together
- Removing departmental barriers
- Improving cross-functional communications
- Enabling greater collaboration between geographically distributed employees
- Linking remote offices
- Changing the nature of work and employment
- Reshaping power structures and management

Big wins often gained through the implementation of organisation-wide Intranets are not dissimilar to those claimed by Silicon Graphics:

> '...the intranet saves £90,000 each day in print and distribution costs, £220,000 per year in training and £45,000 in HR administration each year.'
> (Mansell-Lewis, 1998a)

Chapter 2

Models for implementation

As mentioned previously in this chapter, Intranets are generally recognised as being fairly uncomplicated to initiate. This is especially true if the underlying network infrastructure already exists. However, it is at this point that many corporate Intranets have been seen to stagnate and subsequently fail. So what are the reasons for this?

Following a field study of Intranet implementation in large Danish and South African organisations, Damsgaard and Scheepers (2000) have prescribed a four-stage model that allows an organisation to reflect on each process used to implement their Intranet and plan more strategically for its future development. An inherent benefit in the use of this model is that it provides an opportunity to guard against possible reasons for failure that often occur at these critical stages of implementation.

The four stages of this progressive model towards organisation-wide acceptance of the Intranet are:

Initiation   →   Contagion   →   Control   →   Integration

The authors argue that specific objectives must be fulfilled during each stage of an Intranet's implementation. If these objectives are not met the development of the Intranet will not be able to move to the next stage, resulting in stagnation and it's eventual regression to an experimental system. The objectives for each of these stages are listed in figure 1.

Figure 1. A progressive model for Intranet development

Stage	Objective
1. Initiation:	Identify and recruit a 'sponsor'
2. Contagion:	Achieve critical mass
3. Control:	Establish procedures and standardisation
4. Integration:	Seamless user-access to the corporate memory across the organisation

The generic headings used in the Damsgaard and Scheepers study to describe these stages of implementation have also been used as a logical means of structuring the layout and organisation of the chapters in this book. However, it should be acknowledged right at the start that processes and experiences in real life do not necessarily fall neatly within the sequence of these headings and that a minor number of some topics covered could be mapped onto one or more of the section headings.

With this poetic licence in mind, Part V has been named *Pervasion* as a way of introducing discussion as to what next progressive stage may possibly follow the integration stage, as the next generation of Intranets begins to evolve. To help inform the discussion, the chapter reviews the latest Information and Communication Technologies that are being developed and visions held for the future of work practices in general.

Stage 1: Initiation

At this initial stage the Intranet may be in the form of a feasibility study, a single experimental project or series of emergent 'child' or 'grey' (Ogg, 1997) Intranets dispersed randomly across the organisation. Each discrete 'Intranet island' will often have its own respective 'champion' eager to promote its worth to those in the local vicinity or department.

Therefore, a 'sponsor' is required at this stage to 'adopt or grab' the Intranet(s) to nurture and encourage its growth and usage. These will be prominent members of the organisation and will have the authority to secure funding and the resources to scale out and market the Intranet to the rest of the organisation.

This advocate of the corporate Intranet has been described by Digitext, the Intranet consultancy, as charged with the following remit (Hobbs, 1998):

- to spread the word
- reconcile management with local Intranet managers (department-level Intranet administrators)
- maintain an awareness of high-level company representation as it should be reflected on the Intranet
- encourage user participation by active and overt use of Intranet features such as newsgroups, discussion boards and so on

Chapter 3

Costing your intranet

After careful consideration of the issues in the previous sections and the various options, applications and strategies open to your organisation, you may wish to estimate firstly, the cost of implementing such a project.

Costing the implementation of an Intranet can be tricky not least because of the number of organisations who already have many of the basic components necessary for a basic Intranet. Many employees may also be supporting the development of existing 'grey' Intranets. It is also useful to plan ahead for the almost certain demand for the integration of business-critical applications and legacy systems. These demands will also be accompanied by the costs for maintenance of ever-increasing volumes of information requiring greater investment in both the sophistication of the technology needed and the human resources dedicated to its support and development.

A formula for the costing of human resources is the most complex and will depend largely on the culture of the organisation. It will also depend on the amount of expertise that already exists in the organisation and whether consultants and/or outsourcing are required. Day-to-day management and development should also be costed in terms of whether the Intranet is to be managed centrally by dedicated teams, or whether the responsibility of applications, content and respective budgets are to be devolved to individual departments instead.

However, two areas of costing which are considerably easier to pin down are those associated with the technology and with training.

The following checklist taken from The Corporate Intranet Resource (1998) has been adapted as a method for identifying specific areas of cost. When identifying items of expenditure, initial and ongoing costs should both be taken into account for the following:

Client server costs (i.e. the workstation):
TCP/IP stack
Browser software
Machine upgrades
    CPU
    Memory
    Hard Disk

Operating system
Other components such as multimedia etc.

Server set-up costs:

Web server hardware
Web server software
    Licensing fee
    Installation
    Support contracts
    Other server software
    Server management
    News server
    Mail server
    Proxy server
    Access/user authentication
    Search engine
    Database support
    Log analyser
    Discussion/groupware
    Chat/instant messenger software
    Document management systems
    Intelligent agents
    Portal kits

Networking infrastructure:

Increased bandwidth, routers, Internet Service Providers, cabling upgrades

Content creation:

HTML editors
Graphics editors
Multimedia suites including video streaming software
Java tools
Javascript tools
VBScript tools
ActiveX components
Perl scripts
CGI scripts
Applications

Training costs:

Intranet end-user training
Intranet publishing/authoring training

Application development
Server maintenance
Helpdesk
Other

3.1 Calculating Returns-On-Investment (ROIs)

This section examines and adapts a simple method of calculating ROI as used by the Remedy Corporation (Billings, 2000) and then presents a case study of how the formulae can be applied in practice.

When comparing ROI methods the following calculations may be taken into account:

- Return as a percentage of Investment over fixed period: (Return / Investment) x100

- Return after deducting Investment for a fixed period: (Return - Investment)

- How long until Return equals Investment: (Investment / Return per week)

To use any of the methods above, both potential costs (investment) and savings (returns) first need to be identified. The following bullet points highlight such examples.

Costs (investment)

One time costs:

- Development costs
- Cost of any new software
- Cost of any new hardware

Ongoing costs:

- Information update costs
- Maintenance costs
- Training costs

Savings (returns)

When identifying sources of return, the following may often provide evidence of cost savings:

- Savings through shorter task time
- Savings through shorter processing time
- Savings through the prevention of 'leakage'

'Leakage' here may be defined as those factors often associated with human error that may not otherwise be considered an issue if an automated process was in place. Examples may include misplacing paper-based documents, forwarding incomplete documentation (i.e. omitted authorisation signatures etc.), misinterpreting or miscalculating data (especially during laborious routine work).

Methods used in calculating such cost savings listed above may include:

- Observe old process
- Observe new process
- Make sure to include all phases of both methods
- Measure process times for both
- Check for any statistical differences in outcome
- Measure frequency of task
- Understand fully loaded employee cost per hour

3.2 ROI Case study

Web-based central department diary Vs hard copy version

The Careers Service at Lancaster University offers a number of services that operate in parallel to each other on a daily basis. The wide provision of services demands a significant amount of flexibility from a limited number of staff to ensure these services run smoothly. Areas of provision include reception, enquiries (telephone, email, web-based and face-to-face), scheduled guidance appointments, learner support, workshops, employer visits and meetings, project work (off and on-campus), and regular promotional activities. The majority of staff can be expected to be involved in delivering or supporting any combination of these services depending on the specific commitments that have been previously agreed upon for colleagues that particular day. The key component, that ensures the appropriate staff member is available to deliver these services as effectively and smoothly as possible, is a central (single) department diary.

The system would work by noting all appointments or timetabled staff activities and annual leave notifications in a central hard copy diary. The diary was located centrally in the Careers Service general office as the most convenient place for members of staff to enter, edit and view all entries. Entries for the current day were photocopied and distributed to each member of staff every morning, to be used as quick reference sheets in their respective work areas or offices.

Disadvantages of the system included:

- as soon as someone amended the entry in the central diary for that respective day, the distributed single sheets were then outdated and incorrect
- if someone wished to make a new entry in the diary for a future appointment, for most members of staff this meant leaving their work space or offices and walking to the general office. This could then be complicated further if the individual was:

- off-campus and / or in a meeting and needed to consult the diary (this became even more problematic if the need arose outside normal working hours)
- arranging a convenient appointment date on the telephone
- and / or someone else was currently using the diary at the same time
- and / or they were delayed en-route by a colleague or client

Consequently a business case was made recently for the adoption of an electronic diary in order to alleviate these problems. Unfortunately, the groupware currently used by the service, and those alternative proprietary products available on the market, were insufficiently flexible to meet the specific needs of the department for this purpose. For this reason an in-house web-based solution was sought.

In using the simple examples cited previously, the ROI for this particular case study is illustrated below.

Hard copy diary costs
Editing / checking diary:

Walk to office and edit diary (av. once / day @ 5 minutes per trip):

238 (individual employee working days) x 10 (staff) x 5 (minutes) = 198 hrs

Total: 198 (hours) x £28 (labour costs per hour) = £5,544.00

Delays ('leakage'):

Assuming that for every '1-in-10' trip to the General Office the diary is already in use by another colleague, or the individual is delayed on-route, then a minimum of one additional trip is required (in reality this is likely to involve more trips especially in term-time).

238 (individual employee working days) x 5 (minutes) = 19.8 hrs

Total: 19.8 (hours) x £28 (labour costs per hour) = £554.40

Photocopying:

Master copy: 268 (Careers Service working days) x £0.05 = £13.40
Daily 'personal' copies: 268 (days) x 10 (staff) x £0.05 = £134.00
22 hrs (copying time) x £28 (labour costs per hour) = £616.00

Total: £13.40 + £134.00 + £616.00 = £763.40

Total operating costs per annum: £5,544.00 + £554.40 + £763.40 = £6,861.80

Proposed web-based diary costs
Editing / checking diary:

3 'mouse-clicks' and type in entry (av. once / day @ 30 seconds per entry):
238 (individual employee working days) x 10 (staff) x .5 (minutes) = 19.8 hrs

> *Total:* 19.8 (hours) x £28 (labour costs per hr) = £554.40

Delays (not applicable)

Photocopying (not applicable)

Training (one time only cost):

15 (members of staff) x 15 (minutes) = 3.75 hours;
1 (instructor) x 15 (members of staff) x 15 (minutes) = 3.75 hours;

> *Total:* 3.75hrs + 3.75hrs x £28.00 (labour costs per hour) = £210.00

System development

Creation of HTML templates and interface: 2hrs x £28.00 = £56.00;
Perl script to automatically generate diary pages: 2hrs x £28.00 = £56.00

> *Total:* £56.00 + £56.00 = £112.00

Total operating costs per annum: £554.40 + £210.00 + £112.00 = £876.40

Savings (annual operating costs)
Referring to the previous calculations, the following savings (per annum) can be identified in favour of adopting the proposed web-based diary:

> £6,861.80 (hard copy diary costs) - £876.40 (web diary costs) = £5,985.40

ROI calculations
Return as a percentage of Investment over a fixed period:

- (Return / Investment) x 100
- £5,985.40 / (training + system development costs) x 100
- £5,985.40 / £322.00 x 100 = 1859%

Return after deducting Investment for fixed period:

- Return – Investment
- £5,985.40 - £322.00 = £5,663.40

How long until Return equals Investment:

- Investment / Return per week
- £322.00 / (£5,985.40 / 52) = 2.8 weeks

Calculating the ROIs of such Intranet applications and processes above are relatively straightforward. This is due to the explicit factors relating to time and motion being easily identified, observed and therefore measured. Despite the case study being a relatively simple example, it still provides an insight as to how the early pioneers of Intranet deployment could lay claim to ROIs of a 1,000 percent and more (Campbell, 1996).

Less tangible areas of Intranet ROIs are those benefits that are derived from the adoption of more effective collaborative working and knowledge sharing practices. These factors are inherently difficult to measure due to the implicit way in which each individual absorbs information or knowledge which is then rationalised with their existing knowledge, resulting in new knowledge or ideas being formed, that may then be shared with others (employees, business partners or customers). Xerox is just one example of an organisation that has managed to quantify the benefits gained through Knowledge Management initiatives implemented through Intranet applications (*see* case study – chapter 6.)

Chapter 4

Outsourcing

Outsourcing or sub-contracting work relating to the creation and development of your Intranet can of course be sought at any stage of its evolution. Unfortunately, external consultants or sub-contracting agencies rarely come cheap. Therefore, it is better to recognise at the beginning, especially at the costing phase, as to what services or expertise the organisation has at its disposal and to assess realistically what expertise it is lacking. Attention at this stage should be given to the word 'disposal'. A sponsor or equivalent may have asserted that SQL programming expertise is required (perhaps for integrating legacy databases with a web-browser front-end), then identified a programmer or team of programmers and assumed they will be available for this purpose, without consulting the unsuspecting department or employee. To some it may seem a little unrealistic that a project could be initiated without taking into consideration these kinds of issues. However, due to the way Intranets can be readily implemented and apparently appear inexpensive to set-up, there is still a misconception that many duties and remits relating to the Intranet can be simply subsumed by existing service departments and their respective members of staff.

Even where there is a valid argument that some processes, for instance publishing, will become less work-intensive and therefore free-up time for the employee, there will still be a period of transition whilst the new process replaces the old. This can, in effect, increase the workload of many employees involved in the initiative.

Where resources may first appear to be available for Intranet development, on closer inspection those areas such as IT support may already be overstretched to capacity. Therefore this expertise will need to be sought elsewhere.

Hence the need for a complex financial business plan. Buying in expertise at the very beginning, purely to provide feasibility costings in terms of software needs and human resources, may pay significant dividends in the long run and help avoid unnecessary comprises and embarrassment caused by the underestimation of future costs.

So how can outsourcing help?

First off, unless your staff members have designed an Intranet before, it is unlikely you will have the in-house experience to develop an Intranet. This becomes even more apparent particularly when considering that the implementation of an Intranet requires a wide range of practitioners including project managers, graphic designers, network and security specialists, database specialists, knowledge and information managers and marketing professionals, to name but a few. In contrast a reputable consultancy firm will have built up a stock of such expertise and related associates and may often have applied this knowledge several times over. A consultancy may therefore be able to help you to address and answer the following issues surrounding Intranet development:

- Aims & objectives – what is its purpose?
- Design – what will it look like?
- Processes – how will content be developed and maintained?
- Standards – how will content be managed?
- Technology – what hardware and software is needed and what can you afford?
- ROI – how can you measure Return On Investment?

Different consultancies offer different levels of expertise. This is reflected in the services they offer and not surprisingly in the arguments they provide as to why you should listen to them and not to other consultancies and their advice. At the most basic there are one or two-person bands which will act as a broker to work in your 'best interest' in deciding what areas of expertise you should buy in and why. At the opposite end of this extreme is the sub-contracted agency, which will design, build and take on the overall responsibility of managing your Intranet. Such players include the likes of IBM and Cap Gemini.

In-between these two extremes, the likes of TMS Consulting exist who offer support from conception to implementation (TMS Consulting, 2000). Their design and development methodology prescribed to customer organisations consists of the following stages in Figure 2.

Figure 2. Staged methodology for Intranet implementation

Stage	Description
1.	Project definition: define the objectives of the Intranet and develop a conceptual design for the Web site
2.	Functional prototype: provide a proof of the design concept, agree the look and feel of the Web site, demonstrate functionality, and identify software needed to implement the Intranet
3.	Complete development: complete the development of user functionality, including implementation of software, develop conversion processes and maintenance processes
4.	Populate site: develop and convert static information to populate the site, together with supporting graphics etc.
5.	Deployment: the rollout of an Intranet to users should be supported by training for information providers and users, and an awareness programme publicising the Intranet

Tips sourced elsewhere that claim to help in the process of successful outsourcing, include (Warren, 2000):

DO:

- Think about how long you want the agreement to last; longer deals will be less expensive but you will lose flexibility
- Group services together logically when selecting outsourcing and avoid creating areas where different outsourcers have joint responsibility
- Develop an in-house team with the right skills and enough resources for renegotiations of service level agreements and implementing changes
- Include the people who will manage the contract on a day-to-day basis in contract negotiations – to help minimise the risk of committing to something unrealistic
- Get professional legal advice
- Raise potential service issues early before they become critical

DON'T

- Outsource a problem area
- Skimp on the resources required during the transition period and on an ongoing basis to manage the contract
- Keep staff in the dark about the deal and what will happen to them

- Allow the boundaries of the contract to creep – make sure the contract scope is tightly defined

- Allow purchasing specialist involved in contract negotiations to push you into a cost-reduction deal at the expense of original objectives such as improved service levels

Anyone doubting the market interest in Intranet consultancy services may be interested in a recent report by Datamonitor. The report claims that the European Intranet services market that was valued at $728 million in 1999, is set to rise to over $1.5 billion in 2003.

Datamonitor consultant Philip Codling comments:

'Intranets are the first step along the e-business pathway. Service companies which develop Intranet business practices, will go on to lead the e-business field.'

(Datamonitor, 1999)

So who are the players driving this market?

In the Intranet services field traditional IT service providers such as Cap Gemini and PricewaterhouseCoopers are now competing head-on with major telecommunication companies like BT.

On the whole Datamonitor claim that the following market sectors (figure 3) are all vying for a piece of the substantial pickings that the Intranet services market is predicted to offer:

Figure 3. Converging ICT market sectors and Intranet service providers

Market sector	Intranet service providers
Professional & management services	KPMG, PWC, Ernst and Young, etc.
Telco's and ISPs	BT, C&W, Global One, UUNet, etc.
New Web/Internet specialist companies	Commerce 1, IXL, TMS Information Solutions, USWeb, etc.
Systems integrators	Cap-Gemini, Siemens, Unisys, Wang, etc.
Large IT vendors	Compaq, IBM, etc.

Part II

Contagion

Chapter 5

Achieving Critical Mass

Stage 2: Contagion

The balance between content and the number of users is considered critical to help aid self-proliferation and sustainability for the Intranet. The sponsor's key role at this stage is to 'sell' the Intranet to the organisation and its employees and encourage their own contribution to the expansion of the content.

In a recent benchmarking survey of intranets conducted by the Knowledge Development Centre at Cranfield University (Cap Gemini and Cranfield University, 1999) evidence was found also suggesting that the existence of 'critical mass' is a key factor as to whether an Intranet will provide increasing value to a business.

The three key areas in which 'critical mass' is purported to be required are:

• Users (success can only come from people using the Intranet)
• Content (there has to be ever-more useful and relevant material available)
• Utilisation (the extent to which potential users are connected per day)

The study estimates that at least 40 percent of all potential users need to access the Intranet to achieve this critical mass if real business value is to be generated.

One of the most effective ways of ensuring the Intranet is used regularly and by the majority of employees is to take popular or essential services and ensure that the Intranet is the only means of accessing this area of provision. Such basic tactical considerations may include the publishing of the organisation's newsletter or canteen menu only on the Intranet.

Taking advantage of the multimedia capability of the web browser interface can only increase the popularity of the new medium compared to the paper-based format. Even if some users resort to printing off the newsletter, the frequent use of video-footage and hyperlinking to related resources will help the Intranet version to be perceived as a value-added version of its hard copy predecessor.

Chapter 6

Barriers to Access

Access points

To guard against previously mentioned publishing policies becoming barriers to gaining access to such information, the organisation must ensure that the information is not only available across all workstations but also provide access to the Intranet in all public areas throughout the organisation.

Employees gather, talk and share information in every conceivable location of an organisation – some instances are formally arranged as in the case of a business meeting, whilst others are informal and may take place in a canteen for example.

The content of the discussion may either be related to business matters, whilst others may relate more to personal interests such as inter-department sport or social events.

Regardless of the subject matter, providing instant access in the local vicinity to related information can only bolster the perceived value of the Intranet as the corporate memory and therefore help to achieve the critical mass needed to ensure its success.

Providing kiosks and workstations in areas such as rest areas, reception, canteens, meeting rooms, and near drink and snack vending machines will only help to normalise the culture of seeking information on the Intranet, whether it is checking the departmental diary in a meeting or checking the inter-departmental 'Squash league' during a coffee break!

Cultural aspects

Resistance to change is associated with any move to introduce new software and/or a radically different way of doing business than has gone before. The mere aspect of change and therefore imposed transition of working practices is enough to make the average employee perceive the action to be a potential increase to their personal workload. This is a typical threat perceived by the worker. A more politically sensitive aspect of change is when employees see change as undermining their responsibility or overall power-base in both the organisation and in the immediate structure of their business function.

The conventional notion that 'knowledge/information is power' may often be seen by departmental managers as a means of securing their position in the organisation and ensuring they maintain control over their respective subordinates. This personal position may not be conscious, but may be bolstered by a conditioning of the mind. This can be backed by over-zealous information security policies, convincing the individual that they are merely protecting the intellectual property of the organisation.

For the organisation successfully to share, utilise and create new knowledge, the manager has to be convinced that power does not lie in the protection of the information. True power lies in the ability to share and distribute information.

To nurture this mindset and encourage the sharing of information, organisations need to develop ways of rewarding such electronically-enabled social behaviour. Educational programmes highlighting the worthiness of information sharing and reward schemes formally integrated into appraisal schemes will help employees to recognise that the organisation is truly committed to supporting such a sweeping change in culture. Alongside objectives to improve productivity and business processes, personal objectives should be required to pursue initiatives to disseminate information more widely. Measures should be applied such as the monitoring of retrieval 'hits' to the department Intranet web site or feedback received centrally as to the usefulness of the site reported by users.

A case study: Xerox

The document management firm Xerox, is one company in which creating a knowledge-sharing culture was essential due to the company's workforce becoming increasingly mobile. Working either at home or on the road, many of the company engineers were becoming isolated from their fellow workers and therefore denied access to the friendly advice, experiences and knowledge of others. The opportunity to solve problems collaboratively had also been dramatically reduced.

To alleviate this problem, the company created a web-based knowledge management system christened Eureka that first went 'live' in 1997. The system was designed as a central 'soft knowledge' repository to enable engineers to share problem-solving tips and the kind of tacit knowledge often only stored in the heads of the individual workers.

Eureka was accessed via a standard web browser requiring nothing more than a password to gain entry to the system. This allowed employees to use it anywhere.

Indeed, later research revealed that more than half of all users accessed Eureka from home.

The company quickly realised that, in order to ensure employees continued to use the system, contributions from the engineers themselves would be needed, to help keep the contents up-to-date and relevant. The problem presented to the system managers was: How do you motivate workers to submit useful information at the end of a long shift?

Initially, Xerox offered a bonus of $25 for each piece of information submitted that was not already in the company manual. However, 35,000 tips later the company decided they needed to take a less expensive tack!

The alternative approach proved to be simply to allow employees the reward of being acknowledged. It was realised that employees would still contribute to Eureka, without the financial incentive, if they were recognised as the contributors of their respective submissions with their name appearing on the system.

Xerox claim that Eureka is now so successful that it has moved beyond the realm of the 1,000 UK engineers and 18,000 engineers world-wide, to include the analyst, finance, logistics and finance departments. Three years on from its inception, Xerox claim that Eureka is making a 5 percent difference to bottom-line performance.

Tangible benefits gained from knowledge management or knowledge sharing initiatives are often considered notoriously difficult to measure. So from where was this 5 percent figure derived?

Chris Wise, a European technology manager for Xerox says:

> 'We compare those engineers who have access to Eureka with those who don't and look at issues such as how many spare parts have been ordered, how much time is spent on each job and how many times each engineer has to return to a job.'

(Bentley, 2000)

From a cultural perspective, some do's and don'ts of Intranet implementation to be considered include:

- Fully understand the employee's expectations and requirements
- Be very clear about what the Intranet can deliver
- Take a long-term view about content delivery, but think short-term about encouraging use of the Intranet
- Look for interesting opportunities to tie the Intranet into employee's work
- Make sure it is easy to use

- Involve everyone at all stages
- Don't promise the earth – honesty will gain you credibility in the long term
- Don't ever assume anything
- Empower users with the ability to contribute
- Update the system daily – it must always have something fresh (Intranet Academy, 1999)

At this stage of an Intranet's evolution it is clear that the end-user's confidence in the reliability of the content has to be gained. They will also require an interface that is easy to use. In establishing a commitment on the end-users behalf and ensuring they return to the Intranet, certain factors can be identified that may help ensure progress in these areas. These factors will include (Curry and Stancich, 2000):

- How up-to-date the information is
- The proportion of broken or non-active links that exist
- Organisation and ease of navigation
- Presence of a named contact or not
- Format and content presentation
- Whether new content is in evidence or not
- The speed at which the information loads

Chapter 7

Information supply and retrieval

Publishing content onto an Intranet server does not necessarily ensure that critical mass is achieved. Obviously a means needs to be provided to enable the users to access this information or a complementary method of proactively sharing this information. Therefore, this chapter will look at some of the issues and tools available to support the learner in navigating and retrieving an Intranet's content.

In the following sections, technologies will be reviewed that use specific models of information provision. These forms of information models are applied both in the physical world and via electronic methods of dissemination and are known as 'Pull' and 'Push'. As there is still considerable debate as to which methods should be used, or when one model is more appropriate than another, it is worth at this point clarifying the differences between the two.

A 'Pull' model is an approach to information provision that requires the user specifically to make a request for a piece of information and retrieve or 'Pull' it from a central repository.

In contrast, a 'Push' model approach is where a third party deems that a piece of information is suitable for a given user or group and dispatches this information regardless of whether it has been requested or not.

Benefits are seen in both approaches. The 'Pull' model is useful to the user requiring a specific piece of information at a specific time and not wanting to be delayed looking through irrelevant information. The 'Push' model provides the user with information that may be of interest and of which they would not otherwise have been aware.

The following technologies provide examples of both 'Pull' and 'Push' approaches to information provision.

Search engines

Just as search engines are one of the most popular ways of searching the Internet, by using combinations of keywords chosen by the user, so they have become one of the most popular retrieval technologies available to search an Intranet. In fact, the majority of search engine services on the Internet, including examples such as Altavista [http://www.altavista.com] and Excite [http://www.excite.com], now also produce Intranet versions of their WWW variants and can be expected to provide the same comprehensive range of search facilities including:

- Natural language searching
- Boolean searching
- Automatic root expansion
- Proximity searching
- Numeric searching
- Term-weighted searching
- Thesaurus integration
- Search by object e.g. PowerPoint files, GIF images, Adobe Acrobat files etc
- Search by metadata fields e.g. function categorising, author, date, etc.
- Concept searching e.g. 'find similar to this'
- Summarising facilities

If you are considering using the above list as benchmarking criteria in selecting a search engine product, for your own Intranet, you may wish to consider asking some of the following additional questions as devised by Stenmark (1999) for evaluating search engines for the Volvo Group:

- Is the product designed for [an] Intranet?
- How large are the data volumes that can be handled?
- Can remote web servers be indexed?
- What is coming in the next 6 -12 months?
- What formats other than HTML can be indexed by default?
- Are duplicate links automatically detected?
- How can the crawling be restricted [security issues]?
- Is the index updated in real-time?
- Is the full-text or subset indexed?

The application of Knowledge Management initiatives, through the corporate Intranet, is principally concerned with the distribution of information and enhancing means of access to knowledge resources. There are however, times when restrictions are needed to be placed on access to certain types of information. This should be kept in mind when implementing search engine facilities. Sensitive information that is intended for limited access only, may be inadvertently indexed by the search engine. As a consequence, those using search terms that are contained within these respective documents may then accidentally retrieve it. Technical 'controls' can easily be put in place to block search engines indexing these areas or by limiting the ability of unauthorised users to retrieve these particular documents.

Intelligent agents

Agents are personalised pieces of software designed to search and retrieve information for individual users who do not have the time continually to monitor the wealth of information and knowledge resources available on the Intranet and/or Internet. The word 'intelligent' is used to describe the software's ability to generate sets of rules that are used to refine the user's search criteria into concepts. This allows the agent to determine the context in which keywords are used, to confirm a retrieved document's relevance and to dismiss those sources that are irrelevant to the user.

Vendors of such agent software will obviously provide definitions of such technology that best match the functionality of their own product(s). One criterion that is agreed upon, across these definitions, is that agents possess a significant degree of autonomy compared to traditional client software.

> 'Essentially, intelligent agents are self-contained chunks of mobile code which can act autonomously, respond to changes in their environment and communicate with users or other intelligent agents. Ideally, they also have the ability to learn, or at least be trained.'

> (Mortleman, 2000)

The French telecommunications giant, Alcatel, includes additional characteristics that can be held by agents, besides delegation and autonomy, namely:

> '...rationality, proactiveness, reactiveness, adaptiveness, planning, social ability, reasoning, trustworthiness, user or environment modelling, knowledge base and mobility.'

> (Carrez, 1999)

Whether a vendor lays claim to its product possessing these traits will depend on what type of agent it is. A variety of agents exist, programmed to serve specific business roles. These range from electronic commerce agents (seeking and negotiating business purchases) to personal travel assistants programmed to organise business trips on behalf of the user (including ticket purchases, car rental and hotel reservations).

From a knowledge and information management perspective, the biggest impact that agent technology has made on the business world is in the area of information retrieval. These types of agents are now commonly found bundled in more comprehensive information software systems such as Portals and are examined in more detail in the following section.

Portals

To a certain extent, the previous retrieval technologies highlighted so far can be found in one generic information retrieval (IR) and management product, known as a Portal.

A more familiar example of a portal is the format used by web-based search engines and directories, such as Yahoo!, providing indexed and 'in-context' keyword searching of Internet resources.

The interest in the context of this chapter is with its Intranet cousin, the Enterprise Information Portal (EIP). The EIP, also described as a 'door-way into Intranets' (Computer Technology Research Corporation, 2000), is a web-based interface providing a single point of entry or gateway to an organisation's electronic information resource, using taxonomy common to the enterprise, to classify and organise resources. This eases the IR process for the end-user and also can include the integration of links to Internet resources relevant to the organisation's business needs.

Definitions relating to the purpose of EIPs usually vary, depending on the functionality provided by the portal. Detlor (2000) takes a relatively broad view of their purpose and describes a corporate portal 'functioning as an underlying Web infrastructure for information management' as a 'shared information space that facilitates access to information content, organisational communications, and group collaboration.'

In a recent report the National Computing Centre (Computer Technology Research Corporation, 2000) highlighted the most significant benefits of enterprise portals as:

- Leveraging Intranets and extranets. The portal aggregates, categorises, and delivers pertinent content to critical business audiences while lowering operating costs, increasing sales, facilitating better customer service, and making the supply chain more efficient.

- Built-in security. Because individual users must be authorised, enterprise portals offer another level of security.

- Support of multiple corporate functions. The enterprise portal unifies disparate parts of the enterprise, including accounting, forecasting, and marketing.

- Competitive advantage. Without an enterprise portal, valuable information is locked away in poorly integrated data repositories. Only companies that can access timely information on markets, sales performance, and customer satisfaction via an enterprise portal can develop an advantage over competitors.

With such promises it is not surprising then that the Gartner Group predicts that more than half of all major organisations will be using enterprise portals as the primary method for organising and retrieving organisa-tion-wide information resources by the end of 2001. (Verity, 1999).

The EIP is something again that is new in name but not in concept (Blackmore, 1997a; Hendriks and Vriens, 1999). By 1995 Wirral Metro-politan College was already providing a hierarchical subject-based menu as the default web browser homepage for 1,500 workstations. This pro-vided an optional filter providing access to several hundred web sites, which had been inspected and deemed of suitable quality and relevance for the staff and students of the institution. This system of menus also provided a signpost to the more popular and multimedia enhanced sites mirrored on the College Intranet servers.

Despite being easy to create in-house, due to the intuitive technology un-derlying the web-interface, maintaining such IR facilities in checking, adding new resources and expanding thesauri every day can be extremely labour-intensive and therefore costly. One solution is to buy in one of the new generations of Portal kits such as Autonomy's 'Portal -in-a-Box'™ or Verity's Portal Product Suite.

Common features of these products are the provision of automatic catego-risation and hypertext linking of both structured (i.e. Lotus Notes, ODBC databases, MIS systems) and unstructured data (i.e. PDF, Wordprocessed documents, Emails, PowerPoint presentations, Newsfeeds and electronic journals etc). Other components include personalised Portal interfaces that automatically generate profiles of user interests and complementary search routines, so that they may be regularly alerted to new items of interest or other colleagues with similar profiles, as and when the infor-mation becomes available.

The latest multinationals to adopt portals as the default enterprise-inter-face to their corporate networks are BP and Ford (Adshead, 2000). Both companies have opted for products supplied by Plumtree, the corporate portal supplier.

BP-Amoco is rolling out 'Edesk' to be used by over 50,000 end-users as a single web-based gateway to all the company's popular desktop applica-tions and information resources. Ford has configured the content and applications of its portals according to the job function of specific groups of employees. So for instance, their engineers will be provided with ac-cess to ordering data, materials and component test results.

Plumtree runs on Windows NT but also requires Internet Information Server 4.0 and a suitable database application such as Oracle 8 or MS SQL Server 7.0. However, these additional costs are shadowed by the initial cost of integrated portal systems such as Plumtree starting at around $100,000 for 50,000 users.

Sainsbury's on the other hand has chosen Verity Information Server to provide its employees and suppliers with a '…new advanced knowledge retrieval facility to access workflow and information sharing systems, as well as information on product availability and promotion planning'. (Walder, 1999).

Essex Police have recently purchased Knowledge Server produced by the UK retrieval software vendor Autonomy (Anderson, 1999a), an intelligent search engine product that is able to search several different repositories of information. The system enables Essex Police seamlessly to search web sites (Internet and Intranet), Lotus Notes files, emails, Portable Document Format files and open database connectivity (ODBC) systems. The major difference between this product and other conventional web-based search engines is that the system automatically generates tags and references for specific content within the documents. Pattern-matching algorithms then allow hyperlinks to be made between related documents regardless of their format.

The US car manufacturer General Motors (GM), has also chosen Autonomy to provide a knowledge management software suite for their 140,000 employees based across the world (Silicon.com, 2000). The contract, reported to be worth $2.2m, is designed automatically to catalogue and index all of GM's information that stretches across 1,000 separate Intranet sites holding a total of more than eight million documents.

However certain quarters of the technical press warn against rushing to adopt these products (Moody, 1999; Rapoza, 2000) in light of the dangers that arose in connection with the recent demise of similar products. 'Push' technologies were equally plausible in terms of the business benefits they claimed to offer but like portal products they were unproven and too many players in the market resulted in vendors quickly going out of business (MacClachlan, 1999).

Portals: purchasing issues

When choosing a portal product, no matter how good the additional 'bells and whistles' may sound, the first things to consider are:

Will the vending company still be around in six months?

and;

What is the scope for future development?

The last thing you want to do, after investing such huge amounts of resources in the world's most open standard, is then to buy a product that ties you into a proprietary situation. Avoid systems that cannot be integrated with your own legacy systems or other future third party products at a later date.

This view is supported by the Giga Information Group, which claims that systems having an open architecture and integration between repositories and applications are the most future-proof (Anderson, 1999b). Giga also suggests that potential purchasers should evaluate the following common components of business intelligence portals:

- Does the product have a common logical metadata repository or the ability to integrate with existing data descriptors?
- Will it integrate easily with existing systems?
- Is a 'publish and subscribe' mechanism included?
- How sophisticated are the search and browse functions?
- Does it include categorising/indexing tools?
- Is the system able to define and administer access for users and groups?
- Will the security facilities cater for both Intranet and extranet applications?
- Can the interface be customised?
- Does the system provide personalisation facilities for individual users?

For those organisations that do not have the necessary expertise or technical backup, but still wish to have their own customised solution, outsourcing the enterprise portal to an application service provider (ASP) may be the answer. The Knowledge First package from Computer Aid is no doubt one of the first of many to provide portal solutions on an ASP-basis, a service that also comes bundled with consultancy and training in the use of the software (Hunter, 2000a).

Figure 4. List of portal product and service vendors

Autonomy Portal-in-a-box http://www.autonomy.com	Plumtree Server http://www.plumtree.com
Corechange Coreport http://www.corechange.com	Portera Serviceport http://www.portera.com
Microsoft Digital Dashboard http://www.microsoft.com	Verity Information Server http://www.verity.com
Oracle http://www.oracle.com	Viador E-Portal Suite http://www.viador.com

Chapter 8

Filling the Intranet

Regardless of any decisions that are finalised in how an Intranet project is going to proceed, those involved previously in implementing such projects will agree that for an Intranet to succeed, it must first attract users and then ensure that they return time and time again.

There are generally considered to be two kinds of content: 'flat', also knows as 'static' content and 'interactive' content. This simple method of categorisation generally reflects the level of technical sophistication of an Intranet in being able to relay the information. Research studies (Cap Gemini & Cranfield University, 1999; August, 1999) have cited three stages in which an Intranet often matures, based on the following distinctive generations of development:

Figure 5. Stages of Intranet maturity

→ Flat or static content (also known as the 'Post-it generation')

→ Interactive content (also known as the 'Use-it generation')

→ Extranet/E-commerce applications ('Sell-it generation')

Flat content

Virtually any networking platform, which is able to run a web browser on a workstation, will support the dissemination of 'flat' or 'static' content. The simplistic ease with which this framework can be installed to deliver static information is by far the most common form in which an Intranet first materialises.

This kind of information is simply held in files (web pages or other standardised documents such as wordprocessed files or spreadsheets, etc) on either a networked file or web server. The information is then retrieved and viewed through the use of a web browser and hyperlinks exactly in the same way as the World Wide Web is navigated.

Examples of flat content include:

- Travel aids, maps, service point locations, etc
- The organisation mission statement, aims and objectives, history of organisation

- Internal contact directories: including basic details, job function, location and email addresses
- Internal newsletters and related business info: share prices, major contract info, messages from the Chief Executive Officer or Managing Director
- Product information: specification and ranges of the organisation's products/services; departmental pages: contact details, functions/remits and activities
- Events calendars: relating to organisation and industry-related events and activities
- Dissemination, and compliance/maintenance of policy and procedures manuals e.g. Health and Safety systems, ISO 9000, BS5750 etc.
- FAQ's (frequently asked questions)
- Recruiting and internal job postings
- Subject specific information may be mirrored from the Internet
- Hierarchical subject menus, portals or quality filters providing organised signposts and live hyperlinks to relevant business sources available on the Internet

Interactive content

Once you have identified or started to fill your Intranet with static content and are satisfied that measures, policies and procedures are in place continuously to improve the management of this information; you may then wish to examine how your organisation may capitalise from more interactive Intranet applications such as:

- Electronic mail
- Educational/training systems
- Helpdesk systems
- Search engines
- Forms processing applications i.e. resource reservation systems for conference rooms, pool cars and office equipment; feedback on official documents, reports and surveys; submission of expense claims; submission of internal order/purchase documentation
- Discussion/conferencing boards/Community of Practices (CoP)

It is important to note here the additional technology that is required for an Intranet to make the progression from being able to provide just 'flat content' to include 'interactive content'. It is possible to implement a 'flat content' Intranet on a client-server based network without using TCP/IP (Internet Protocol) (Blackmore, 1997b) as long as it will support the use of web browsers on its workstations. However, to provide examples of the interactive content listed above, you will need to install a web server. This is software needed to execute the various programmes and 'scripts' required for the provision of interactive and dynamic content.

Commercial or externally-sourced information

- Electronic databases
- Electronic journals
- Electronic newsfeeds

These examples may fall into either category of flat or interactive content depending on the product or service subscribed to or purchased but you may find that the provision of such resources provides an effective 'honeypot' to attract users quickly and to ensure they return frequently.

In researching the subject matter for this chapter, commercial services and products available for populating Intranets with current awareness information were sought. A number of large on-line database providers were surveyed, with regards to their current and future policies on allowing customers to distribute content on their respective Intranets. On the whole most responses were surprisingly reserved. As one senior product manager, who did not wished to be named, commented '…too much time and investment is put into producing our databases for us to then risk the information becoming freely available to all and sundry without charge. Even worse, to risk the content being gleaned by a competitor for their own use.'

Other providers claimed they were currently discussing policy on such use of their products across corporate Intranets, whilst others commented that such arrangements would need to be negotiated between themselves and each individual customer on an individual basis. Those policies that did exist tended to be based upon the number of potential users in the organisation and the time span that the content would be available on the system.

STN on the other hand, the on-line database provider for science and technology information, already has such a service in place that goes by the name of the 'STN Information Keep and Share Programme'. The STN Programme allows clients to purchase the right to archive and redistribute search results retrieved from STN databases. However they highlight that in a minor number of exceptional cases, restrictions are placed on the use of specific database contents.

Chemical Abstracts, containing more than 15 million document records, is one such database producer that understandably has 'acceptable use policies' in place to protect its intellectual property. On closer inspection these policies would seem not to be too restrictive when conditions such as the following apply.

'You may download up to and including 50,000 records of CAS information per year in a database for searching by individuals within your organisation.'

(STN, 2000)

The Dialog Corporation has also recently launched their Intranet Toolkit (Dialog, 2000) offering live access to several thousand databanks via a customised web interface. The difference between this form of access made via the Intranet and the conventional access available to anyone via the Internet is that usage is controlled and managed centrally in the organisation. This remit may be held by a member of the Intranet administration team or a department charged specifically with this role, such as the Library and Information department.

LEXIS-NEXIS, The Business and Industry database provider, also permits use of their information to populate corporate Intranets. Documents from a 60-day news archive can be selected and posted to an organisation's Intranet web servers for up to 90 days.

Business Intelligence information

For those organisations operating in a competitive business climate or market sector, an Intranet may provide more high-profiled returns if the content reflects such information needs. Intranet Design Magazine (2000) provides examples of competitive intelligence information that can be managed and shared on an Intranet. These are categorised as follows:

Organisation: organisational structure with profiles of key and senior personnel

Financial: latest annual reports, quarterly reports, analysis, press releases of financial performance, comparisons with competitor results, projected results

Products: product specifications and comparisons with other products in the range, product images and photographs, technical content, new product releases, patents

Pricing: competitor pricing expectations, regional and international pricing, speculated prices

Alliances: partners and date of formal joint-venture agreements, implications on market and business

Customers: lists of both your company's customers and competitor's customers

Technology: product descriptions and comparisons

Customers: profiles, key business contacts and remits, action lists, approach and customer management strategies, financial status, customer alliances with other businesses and sectors

Regulation: key regulatory texts and interpretation, news of current enforcement cases, future acts and bills pending

Market: actual size of current and forecasted markets, market trends, key economic reports and news items

Customer surveys: key findings of customer surveys, analysis and action plan for the company

Marketing toolkit: latest company and / or product presentations, travel schedules and booking facilities, visitors schedule, database of marketing resources (e.g. images, spreadsheets, graphs, tables etc.)

Jungle phone: rumours, unchecked facts

Suppliers: profiles, product range, Service Level Agreements, relationship strategies

8.1 Legacy Systems

One of the quickest and most effective ways of populating your Intranet with useful information is obviously by using existing information. The more mission-critical the information is in nature, the more likely that the Intranet will be used, especially if access is restricted due to a web interface being the only means of retrieving the information.

The bulk of such data and information held in organisations is contained within database systems, the contents of which are often changed, updated or added to, on a daily basis, and provide a wealth of useful information that can be made available to the organisation.

Examples of such information may include collections of digitised documents, Library Management System catalogues, products and respective price lists, telephone and in-house expert directories, to name just a few resources commonly found in most organisations.

The use of databases can help dramatically improve the effectiveness of processes used for maintaining the currency of an Intranets content. Policing the currency of static web pages may, at the beginning of an Intranets implementation, seem relatively easy. Unfortunately, as content grows, this can become an overbearing task, even in cases where the editorial responsibility has been devolved to the respective individual authors and departments to monitor this area of quality assurance.

From a novice's perspective, there are three general levels of integrating database content with web interfaces:

i]   content generated through auto-generated HTML reports where
        the data is not changing too frequently and no user input is re-
        quired to change the original database records

ii]   content generated 'on-the-fly' providing real-time access to data
        providing more flexible search criteria, access to the most up-to-
        date contents and the ability for users to enter or change data in
        database records where this is permitted

A third level of provision also exists which is a compromise between the
options above, providing the security of maintaining data integrity as in
example i] but with the flexibility of using more complex search criteria as
in example ii]. This third option involves the replicating or copying of the
whole database to a secure area at set intervals, from where it can then be
interrogated by users via a web browser.

This particular option may be especially appealing to those organisations or departments who have significant concerns about maintaining
the integrity of the original database contents, or who feel they do not
have the necessary skills to protect the original database.

Launching legacy systems via web-based menus

Many organisations will have significant amounts of information and
databases provided by commercial information providers. These may include bibliographic databases or full-text resources. Although information
providers are slowly adding web-interfaces to these products, independent software solution vendors are now supplying a means of adding a
web interface to almost any CD-ROM based product. This removes the
need for individual workstations to be configured in order to allow access. Two specific UK-produced products in this market are: Info
Technology Supply Ltd [http://www.itsltduk.com] and UltraNet [http:
//www.fenwood.co.uk]. These products also have metering systems to
allow simultaneous usage to be monitored, so as not to contravene any
licensing agreements with commercial information providers. Despite the
availability of this technology, anyone considering purchasing such a
solution would be advised first to check with the supplier that any third
party content is licensed to be networked in the first place.

Such solutions however can be expensive and may not be a viable option
for many organisations. One way of compromising on such provision is
to use the Intranet to guide the user to a specific resource and then enable
the user to launch the resource rather than run the application through
the web browser itself. This method of launching any application with an
executable file is especially useful for a number of reasons:

•   provides quick point-and-click access to resources and applica-
        tions across the network

- allows disparate resources to be readily located by categorising under meaningful subject headings
- introductory text describing the resource contents can be provided along with signposts to any in-house generated help-sheets or manuals
- provides a means of bringing complementary or alternative sources to the attention of users who may have not been aware of their existence previously
- removes the need for users to navigate, and be familiar with, network and drive mapping procedures

In my own practice at Lancaster University Careers Service we have many applications and software packages available for both staff and students. Many of these include electronic directories, computer-assisted guidance packages and CD-ROM based multimedia resources supplied by graduate employers and other information service providers. All these resources can be found and launched on the Careers Service and University campus Intranet by clicking on their respective links. Each link seamlessly connects to a simple script (i.e. batch file) that maps a drive to the location of the target resource and passes a command for the executable file to run. As far as the user is concerned, the application requires no more skill to launch the application than is required to click on the respective hyperlink.

By its very nature, every compromise obviously has its limitations. In this case, users must be accessing the Intranet via a workstation connected directly to the network.

Convert existing documentation using conversion utilities

Many organisations have thousands of pages of policies and reference material in proprietary format. It is highly unusual for systems these days not to have some kind of utility function for converting or saving them in HTML so that they may be readily published onto the Intranet. Once this is done you may want to consider whether this information needs to be maintained in its original format at all. It may be preferable to maintain all future amendments in HTML.

PowerPoint presentations can also be simply converted into web shows using a minimum number of clicks by the author without any prior knowledge of HTML authoring. With the vast number of PowerPoint presentations available within an organisation, this again is a simple and quick way of populating the content space of an Intranet. Likewise, databases such as Access allow any number of comprehensive reports to be generated quickly into HTML format.

However a health warning should be made with this kind of strategy. As with any kind of 'live' presentations there are good and bad computer-generated presentations and the quality of the overall content of an Intranet should not be compromised by blindly converting all computer-formatted presentations into HTML pages. Whether this control is self-imposed or judged by a third party, basic questions should be asked regarding quality before such information is published on the Intranet. For instance, does the presentation offer value to the organisation as a piece of knowledge or information in its own right, or can notes or some other complementary information be added, such as a summary report of the original presentation? Of course such quality measures can be made much more effective if made explicit in an organisation's publishing policy.

Chapter 9

Business Applications and Services

The following section highlights departments and functions that can benefit significantly from utilising an organisation's Intranet in performing their core business activities. However, it does not suggest that these are the only areas in which this would be worthwhile, in terms of added value, for the organisational Intranet. The more appealing that Intranet content can be made, to a wide cross-section of the organisation, the greater the use and the greater the interest from all related parties, in seeing it succeed and grow.

Unfortunately the scope of this chapter does not allow for a blow-by-blow account of how each business function can exploit the benefits offered by Intranet applications. However, the following examples are given to show how central services may use an Intranet to add business-value to the range and delivery of their core services, many of which may be adopted in other functions across the organisation.

9.1 The Personnel department

Content with instant appeal across all functions of an organisation is obviously a desirable asset and will encourage the successful implementation of an Intranet. One business area that provides such opportunities is the Personnel - or Human Resource (HR) - department.

HR functions are often charged with the remit of publishing and distributing large amounts of documentation across the organisation. Such documents include organisation charts, telephone directories, newsletters, personnel policies and procedures, employee handbooks, training schedules etc.

The added value in these services becoming available organisation-wide is not just in the fact that they are easily accessible, but also in the relative confidence that this information is more up-to-date than any hard copy counterpart.

This dependency of the organisation on such a currency-critical range of information usually results in a huge drain on the financial resources of the HR department in terms of reprographics and distribution costs. However, dissemination via the Intranet removes these costs associated with the hard copy derivative and provides a quality of service that enables timely access to current and accurate information for all employees at the same time regardless of their location.

To many, the cost savings highlighted would seem a strong enough business case in itself to ensure the implementation of an organisation-wide Intranet. Despite the transparency of such benefits, some claim that more significant gains are to be made in HR through the introduction of Intranet systems that enhance the business process (Newing, 1997).

Providing authenticated electronic access to individual personnel records for managers and employees in order to change details such as addresses, telephone numbers, marriages, job descriptions etc., can significantly relieve HR personnel of these routine administrative tasks to pursue more proactive strategic remits.

9.2 Library and Information Services

Strong arguments are often made for the Library and Information Service (LIS) to be at the centre of any programme to roll out new information management or dissemination technology (Blakeman, 1996; Blackmore, 1997b). The same argument can equally be applied to the introduction of Intranets based on the success of many case studies (Bevan and Evans, 1996; Blackmore, 1996; ISAC, 1998; Primich and Varnum, 1999).

A LIS will already possess knowledge of the salient issues and skills required to source, organise and disseminate information to an organisation. The LIS will already have close business relationships with internal customers that span the organisation and have knowledge of their respective information needs. Indeed, in a study of several corporate libraries, it was highlighted that much inconvenience can be saved by involving the information management skills of the LIS at the outset rather than bringing them in to revamp and trouble-shoot once the size of an organisations Intranet has become too unwieldy in later years (Hall and Jones, 2000).

Furthermore, the department will already hold large amounts of information, often in electronic format, ready to add instant and useful content to the Intranet. Depending on the organisation, the LIS may have responsibility for many of the remits described above for the HR department. Services specific to the LIS, which can add instant value to an Intranet include: book catalogue databases, journal catalogues, new acquisitions databases and technical reports databases. Web-interfaced loan systems are able to provide loans and reservations for hard copy resources whilst electronic resources can be quickly accessed through retrieval systems via established and meaningful controlled thesauri. CD-ROMs storing electronic journals and databases can also be launched and viewed via the web browser interface.

9.3 IT department

The department charged with the responsibility of supporting the needs of the end-user and maintaining and repairing hardware is known variously as IT, Computer support, Computing Services or Information Systems and Services and is a central service used by everyone in the organisation and thereby an ideal source of instant content and value-added services for the Intranet.

Services can range from static content such as: software manuals, workstation specifications and purchasing recommendations, Frequently Ask Questions (FAQs), newsletters, lists of software availability, anti-virus alerts and advice, workstation and software configurations, corporate Intranet templates, remote access instructions, security policies, training programmes, staff remits and contact details.

More dynamic content can include forms processing, 'backoffice' databases (for fault reporting, room and equipment bookings, general enquiries etc.) and Knowledge-based Management Systems for on-line help applications.

The additional value gained from adopting web-based helpdesk systems compared to proprietary database solutions can simply arise as a benefit for allowing users to register faults and problems through self-logging systems via the Intranet (Samuels, 2000). Multi-nationals on the other hand, with employees working on disparate corporate sites in different time zones, may use web-based scheduling systems that permit helpdesk queries to be redirected to IT support people based anywhere in the world (Greer, 1998). With sophisticated levels of functionality and security available for remote access via extranets and Intranets, support may be either met by in-house teams or outsourced to third party-managed call centres.

As an example of the extent to which IT support can now be provided using Internet technologies; the Careers Service at Lancaster University recently experienced problems when installing Virtual Learning Environment software to be used to support our on-line Career Development Learning programmes. Following an email requesting assistance, a telephone appointment was arranged with a support engineer of the software vending company. Prior to the call, remote access software was downloaded from the vendor's web site and quickly installed on our host server. Upon receiving the telephone call from the software engineer, he was informed of the server's IP address (machine name) on the University's Intranet and presented with a temporary access password. Seconds later, two technicians and myself stood and watched bemused as the software engineer began to manipulate the cursor and edit key configuration files remotely via the Internet. Within 15 minutes of receiving the phone call, the problem had been resolved, we had uninstalled the remote-access software and finally said our goodbyes to the software engineer sat at his desk in Washington DC!

With such ease of access permitted due to the advent of remote access Internet technologies, maybe it is not so surprising that a survey by the National Computing Centre revealed that 10 percent of UK companies outsource their helpdesk (Samuels, 2000).

9.4 Training, education and e-learning

Not necessarily a central function within an organisation but relevant to all business areas is the provision of training and education. Training, education and professional development have long been recognised as being vital ingredients for modern businesses committed to becoming or remaining a Learning Organisation and wishing to retain and motivate their workforce. Such provision is used as a cost-effective means for increasing productivity throughout the organisation.

Despite this belief, two of the main issues (besides their financial resourcing), which may be seen to hinder initiatives that deliver effective and comprehensive provision of this nature include:

> i] *from the employer's perspective* - as British Aerospace recognises, (Kenny-Wallace, 1999a) time spent by employees on educational programmes is 'business time away from the work place' which is then 'lost time to be made up if production times and design-to-delivery times are not to falter'.

> ii] *from the employee's perspective* - this perspective, although closely related to the above, is mostly concerned with the pressures placed upon employees who may be supported financially by the organisation but whose working hours or shift-patterns may not provide them with the flexibility needed for them to attend classes or training programmes in further or higher education institutions.

In the past, larger employers (educational institutions aside) have tried to alleviate some of these barriers by providing access to Computer-Based Training software packages and audio-visual media resources made available through on-site learning centres. Whilst overcoming some of the related access problems to training, this solution still falls short of the professionally validated courses and qualifications provided by conventional educational institutions. There is also the not-so-insignificant absence of the wealth of dedicated learner support from resource materials, tutors and peers provided by these institutions.

Fortunately, such issues associated with training and education are increasingly being resolved through the use of Intranet/extranet solutions.

At the basic end of provision, in-house or bought-in training materials may be quickly delivered anywhere in the organisation to the employee's desktop any time of day or night. These can be further enhanced by the delivery of multimedia materials supported by Internet technologies such as streaming video, audio and animated Powerpoint presentations. At the other end of the spectrum, sophisticated web-based learning support and provision exist in forms such as the Virtual University run by BAe in partnership with a number of Further and Higher Education Institutions across the UK (Kenny-Wallace, G, 1999a).

One such partnership exists in the form of the British Aerospace Management Certificate with the Open University and Lancaster University, a co-designed programme that includes executive behavioural skills and teamwork.

This programme and others, including MBA studies, is intended to be delivered to some 5,000 employees over the coming years. In justifying such an investment British Aerospace state:

> 'Ultimately, the cost effectiveness of a learning strategy has to include the affordability of such a major investment. Within British Aerospace, we seek economies of scope and scale, of optimum use of employee's time and of the flexibility that episodic learning can offer to different groups of employees whose day jobs present them with different degrees of freedom.'

(Kenny-Wallace, 1999b)

In addressing one of the biggest criticisms of Distance Learning in recent years British Aerospace also comments:

> 'There is no question that, in education, intellectual and social interaction with others is important and this should be a feature of the overall learning experience.'

(Kenny-Wallace, 1999b)

In the Lancaster University partnership, as with other similar programmes with the likes of British Airways, Lancaster is able to support this social interaction between the employees from the same organisation who may be separated by time, working regimes, and location, simply by providing secure 'virtual discussion areas'. Different forums are created to allow the discussion of curriculum, facilitate areas for group project work or provide a virtual space to discuss personal issues and professional developments with their peers and programme tutors.

The company-wide Virtual University Intranet also provides a Learning and Development Guide describing over 2,000 courses and provides advice on learning styles and personal development plans. The guide assists employees with their career progression decisions across 39 sites spread across the UK, Germany, France, Saudi Arabia, Australia and the USA (Kenny-Wallace, 1999c).

The Unipart Group of Companies has also launched its own 'Virtual U', an on-line learning system that aims to deliver electronic courses to 10,000 employees via the corporate Intranet (Unipart, 2000). Course provision includes:

i] 'Learning to use the micrometer' – a course designed to enable anyone to start with no knowledge of using the precision engineering tool and to progress to full competency with an hour's worth of training

ii] 'An introduction to Policy Deployment' – a way of teaching the business process that aligns corporate objectives at every level of the organisation

iii] 'Space management' – a course that teaches effective utilisation of space, which is critical for warehouse and manufacturing environments

All courses can be accessed via the employee's desktop or for those employees who do not typically have access to PCs in their daily work, the Unipart 'U' initiative has provided 'Faculty on the Floor' learning centres located on the shop floors of manufacturing and distribution areas.

Unipart claim that this form of web-based training not only saves up to 80 percent of training time for the new employees but has also freed up the time of experienced engineers who were once responsible for conducting this area of training.

As Corporate Liaison Manager at Wirral Metropolitan College, I was also responsible for managing the provision of direct electronic learner-support through Intranet/extranet feeds to Learner Resource Centres based on-site at companies such as Cadbury's Premier Brands and Vauxhall Motors. This equity in provision with their campus counterparts provided employees with the opportunity to study and attend classes before work, during lunch breaks and at the end of working 'shifts'. Not only does the web-based interface permit the use of multimedia learning materials to provide added stimulus to the learning experience but corporate-based learners also gain access to their tutors more readily via email and discussion boards. Value-added provision is also made, especially when face-to-face access to tutorial support is so limited due to each respective party's restricted work schedules (Blackmore, 1998).

The Bell Atlantic Corporation extends this provision further by providing a purposely designed hybrid web-based learning environment and Knowledge Management System to educate Bell Atlantic technicians for advanced technical positions in the corporation. The 'Next Step Programme' uses a Lotus Notes/Domino based system known to its members as the 'Knowledge Depot System'. The system, in the words of Bell Atlantic, is:

> '…a knowledge management system that facilitates communication and co-ordination among over 2,000 students, faculty and staff in an innovative training programme that involves 25 colleges spread over six states.… Because students work in different places and at different times, face-to-face communication is rare and students use the Knowledge Depot for much of their communication and co-ordination.'

> (Zimmerman et al, 2000)

The value of the system as a Knowledge Management tool is discussed further in the Groupware section.

In implementing its own enterprise web-based training solutions Dow Chemical has also claimed impressive benefits in terms of returns-on-investment. With over 24,000 course completions in 1999, the company claims to have re-couped its initial investment in less than 12 months. Savings over the next three years are claimed to be on track to save $15-$20 million.

Cisco, the multi-national networking corporation, is another company which has reaped significant returns in delivering training via their Intranet to their 10,000 strong army of sales staff based in 150 countries. Taking these employees out of the field and into the classroom costs the company £16 million a week. This is less surprising when taking into account that Cisco buys new companies, on average, every two and a half weeks and every time this happens, there is a need to train sales staff. Through the introduction of an e-learning solution these training delivery costs have been halved in the first year with 80 percent of sales and technology training now provided on-line (Hammond, 2001).

Despite the notable savings experienced, it may not be unreasonable to assume that this sweeping change in culture and the use of technology is more readily achievable in a technology-driven organisation such as Cisco, opposed to those who operate in a more traditional market. However, it would appear that Nestlé (the food multi-national) is one organisation that does not agree with this point of view. In a 12 month contract worth

£1.5 million, just signed with e-learning provider NETg, Nestlé will be delivering training via their corporate Intranet to 200,000 employees worldwide (Rana, 2001).

You may be wondering then, how your organisation might make such impressive savings as those that have been highlighted so far. Dow Chemical gave the following tips to delegates at a recent conference for those contemplating such initiatives:

- Keep it simple
- Basic text and graphics are effective
- Adapt existing instructional content and design
- Plan for deployment
- Zero desktop installations
- Make sure the system you use can scale
- Measure to prove ROI
- Assess skills and improvement over time
- Track usage and effectiveness
  (Walker, 2000)

The latest annual national training survey by the Institute of Personnel and Development (IPD) shows that the value placed on Intranets as a training tool is not limited to just one or two innovative organisations. The previous survey revealed that one-quarter of the 600 companies who took part in the survey provided training via the Internet and Intranets. Twelve months on, the findings reveal a 13 percent growth in the use of the Internet and a 17 percent growth in the use of Intranets (Rana, 2000).

Not surprisingly, the US is heading the drive in turning to e-learning as the most cost-effective training solution with the market in 2000 claimed to have been worth $2 billion. By 2003, this figure is expected to rise to $11 billion (Rana, 2001).

Part III

Control

Chapter 10

Procedures and Standardisation

Stage 3: Control

Once critical mass has been achieved it is essential that relevance and currency of information and data can be guaranteed. If these policies are not in place the following problems begin to arise:

- 'dead' hyperlinks
- dated information becomes misinformation
- lack of cohesion and connectedness between new and existing content
- information overload on the part of the end-user
- navigating and locating content becomes ever more difficult

If this state goes unchecked the user population will start to mistrust the integrity and value of the content, which in turn will quickly lead to ever decreasing states of stagnation.

Additional factors not yet considered as to why Intranets sometimes fail may also include:

- Lack of training – should not just include browser training but also training in the use of all other Intranet software, Boolean searching, and raising awareness of content validation issues
- Unauthorised access (security breaches) to Intranet content via external networks (extranets, VPNs etc)
- Inefficient retrieval tools, thereby creating time wasted through the process of retrieving information and then the problem of noise-to-relevance ratio whilst deciphering what is and what isn't useful
- Bandwidth – do not overload the system and frustrate the end-user with needless bells and whistles i.e. do not use multimedia formats where text will do!
- A misconception (or worse the actual realisation by employees) that the implementation of the Intranet is in some way connected to down-sizing initiatives by senior management
- failure to recognise up-and-coming technologies
- failure to control protectionist behaviour by knowledge holders or information gatekeepers

Chapter 11

Content Management Issues

This next section highlights some of the technologies used to manage the storage and retrieval of the organisation's intellectual assets.

The Internet has often been described as the world's biggest library. Others, presumably information workers (?), have agreed and added '...yes, but with all the books thrown on the floor!'.

The problem with Intranets is that, these too can become just as unwieldy as the Internet to navigate and can provide significant barriers to retrieving desired information. In a recent survey of IT users conducted by the UK National Computing Centre (1999), over half of the respondents regarded the keeping of Intranet content up-to-date as a major problem and one-third also regarded the control of new incoming material submitted by users as a major problem.

As cited in the section describing the life cycle of Intranet implementation, the ease of Intranet publishing can quickly make Intranets appear to be victims of their own success. As with paper-based systems, Intranet content also needs to be organised and maintained effectively. This is not only essential to enable the timely retrieval of information, but maintaining the integrity of information is often a compliance activity when dealing with quality assurance systems or customer projects and may often be subject to stringent auditing procedures.

Ownership of content

Many of the pioneer organisations who first recognised the significant benefits associated with the implementation of an Intranet also had the foresight to realise that it is important to have strict rules about what can and cannot be published on the Intranet. Without control, danger loomed with the opportunity for people publishing irrelevant information on the system, thereby placing needless barriers to searching for information of prime value to the business.

As a measure against this potential chaos arising, organisations first looked to their Webmaster to take charge of the content management of their internal web servers. This did not seem to be such an unreasonable decision especially as this remit had typically belonged to the webmaster in managing the corporate web site in the first place. However, the corporate web site at the time (and which still remains so, in many cases) was used primarily as a marketing tool giving an organisation a web presence to provide an overview of the organisation, its products and services and contact details for further enquiries. With such a limited range of information the management of this content was not, therefore, such a daunting task.

However, take an organisation with several hundred or thousand employees each in a department or section and ask them to identify any mission-critical data or information that they believe will be valuable to other employees across the organisation. Then ask them to forward this information to the webmaster to be processed for inclusion on the organisation's Intranet (and possibly Internet web site). Not surprisingly this scenario would typically result in a backlog of work and email attachments on the desktop of the webmaster! This phenomenon quickly earned the nickname 'webmaster-bottleneck'.

The least business-critical result of such a scenario may be that employees would have to seek the information by other means, perhaps by contacting a relevant department directly. The worst scenario was that critical data or notification of specific deadlines could be out-of-date by the time the information was displayed on the Intranet.

One such problem has been highlighted by Jörg Deibert, vice president of information specialists NovaSoft, who commented on a case in which the price list on a company's Web site was not the same as that quoted by its staff (Mansell-Lewis, 1998a).

As is now commonly seen as the most sensible approach by many organisations experienced in avoiding such situations, Deibert suggests.

> 'Each department needs to have someone responsible for pages and subsections on the Intranet. They have to understand that when information is cross-referenced with another department, it has to be updated.'
>
> (Mansell-Lewis, 1998a).

Tim Coote, senior manager at IT services company Cap Gemini throws further light on what this remit of 'ownership' might entail.

> 'You have to nominate one information owner per knowledge area. They can delegate the writing task to other members but they have to take ultimate responsibility for content and ensure that there is a link in the document that puts any reader back to them if there are content issues.'
>
> (Mansell-Lewis, 1998a).

Scottish Power is one such company preferring to devolve the responsibility for content to specific departments. In using an independent software vendor, ActiveIntranet Plc., Scottish Power sought a solution that would enable individual departments or groups of users to build and run their own Intranets, extranets or Internet web sites. The set-up is claimed to enable non-technical users with a minimal amount of training to maintain and publish Intranet content. Again one of the main advantages is seen as avoiding 'webmaster-bottleneck' meaning that users can post up material instantly rather than wait for weeks for a webmaster to translate documents.

This model is also adopted in my own practice where each of the 12 members of a small department is responsible for the upkeep of their own sections of both the Web site and the Intranet. The information that relates directly to their job is only accessible for editing purposes by the webmaster and themselves who are sanctioned as the respective 'author' responsible for updating this specific information.

Not so long ago the action of transferring a document to a web server required the use of an FTP (File Transfer Protocol) client, username and password to log-on to the server and upload specific files into the server directory. In many cases this still applies. In our own set-up, the read-write access rights for each individual are governed by the same user manager system that controls access rights for all users to all documents. In this case, the user accesses the Permissions function in NT.

Using Netscape Navigator, any member of staff can edit their designated pages within two clicks of the mouse button via the integrated HTML authoring facility 'Composer'. Without any knowledge of HTML authoring, the user may then edit the page and save it to the appropriate directory. As the user is already recognised by the system as a known and trusted member of staff, the file may be simply saved, either in the existing location or elsewhere, as a new page according to whether the user has access rights to that area or not.

Training every member of the Service to amend and save files in this way took less than one hour. Imagine the cost savings in staff time that have been saved compared to the previous manner of changing HTML pages, let alone the lengthy processes involved with changing any equivalent in hard copy format.

Such was the effort by software houses to get new products into this booming market that a term was introduced in recent years to help describe the short time it took from researching and testing a product to its delivery to the public market. Whereas releases of a product version may have typically taken 12 months, these releases were now occurring every three to five months. These periods typically then became known as a web year! So what is the point you may well ask? The point is that technology, especially Internet-related, is especially transient. Organisations should guard against investing hundreds of thousands of pounds in training up staff in the use of sophisticated products that may be replaced in six months or made redundant in 12 months.

Special notice should be given to the use and training of sophisticated HTML-authoring software. This may simply result in a case of over-engineering the process and introducing unnecessary technological barriers to the users. Does your average user who needs to edit simple text really need to know what the script for a 'radio button' looks like?

As with many lessons learned, even with information technology, history can provide an example of this transient nature of technology and the training needed. Take the example of word-processing software. In the early eighties, word-processing systems such as WordPerfect typically required the user to provide brief commands in the document to instruct the software to place something in bold or italics. Now, everyone takes it for granted with WYSIWYG (What You See Is What You Get) standardisations anyone can carry out these same functions using standardised icon-imagery across a range of software applications.

This same transition has occurred in HTML authoring. HTML authoring is not a million miles away from the skills that were once needed in creating a word-processed document; skills that are now redundant. Likewise, whereas word-processing skills were in some cases considered unique, but are now regarded as commonplace; so this should be the same case with editing HTML documents considering the intuitive and simple tools that are now available.

The biggest tip to help guarantee that something technological works across a wide user-base is - always keep it simple!

This section has been mainly concerned with the management of content from the perspective of its organisation so that it may be accessed easily and retrieved by the appropriately authorised users. In other words, the content is destined to be in a static state for a significant period of time in order for the knowledge within to be disseminated to the organisation at large.

Other content or digitised materials exist in an organisation that are frequently in a more dynamic state and are only required to be accessed by a discrete number of relevant employees. The approach to managing the processing of information in this way is referred to as workflow. More details regarding Workflow Management Systems are discussed in the Groupware section.

11.1 Management Structures

This informal approach to devolving ownership of information and subsequent publishing rights can be considered by some organisations to be too 'open' for comfort.

However more formal team-based approaches can still be implemented across an organisation to ensure corporate identity and quality standards are applied consistently, without stifling individual department creativity and enthusiasm for contributing to the Intranet.

This chapter describes two approaches to managing Intranet management structures and key players.

Intranet management structures, example 1.

Digitext, the UK-based Intranet consultancy, claims the most common management structures are made up of the following representatives:

- Webmaster and team
- Local Intranet managers
- Local Intranet developers
- Information owners

Webmaster and team

The webmaster, or central information manager and team, should have responsibility for areas that affect all departments and/or include remits that may not naturally fall into the regular remits of existing departments. Responsibilities typically may include:

- Development, maintenance and policing of standards and templates
- Control and production of top-level or corporate pages
- Management of central web servers, firewalls and Internet access
- Liaison with any external network (including the Internet) providers or related outsourcing
- Promoting and co-ordinating the sharing of best practice amongst local Intranet developers and Intranet managers across the organisation
- Advising of new technologies to other Intranet developers within departments

Local Intranet managers

There should be as many local Intranet managers in an organisation as there are departments or sections. Their remit is to market and encourage the use of, and contribution to, the Intranet by the employees working in their respective local areas. With many responsibilities similar to the webmaster and central Intranet team, they will include:

- Overall policy for their area of the Intranet or their respective Intranet web server
- Co-ordinating their local team of developers and information owners
- Liaison with the central webmaster and Intranet team and cascading relevant information and policies back to developers and information owners in their areas
- Depending on how far security and publishing rights are devolved in local areas, the local Intranet manager may also be responsible for publishing or authorising local content for wider public consumption, either for suppliers or known customers or even for access via the Corporate web site

Local Intranet developers

As the title of this job function may suggest the local Intranet developer is mostly concerned with the technical aspects of information and Intranet service provision. In the smaller department the local Intranet manager and developer may be one and the same person. Their responsibilities should include:

- Developing pages
- Publishing pages to the Web server if authorised
- Ensuring that their local pages conform to organisation-wide standards
- Developing and maintaining integration systems with legacy applications and databases etc.
- Updating pages through collaborating with information providers or providing technical assistance and troubleshooting services to authors who are granted publishing rights

Information owners

Information owners are any employees who would be ordinarily recognised and charged with the responsibility of disseminating or maintaining information regardless of its format. They may be experts and authors in specific knowledge areas, or library assistants charged with allocating technical report numbers to official internal documentation. Regardless of their seniority in the organisation each would have overall responsibility for ensuring this data or information is presented in its correct form on the Intranet. Any feedback on this related content should be fed directly back to the information owners. Then these individuals will liaise with the intranet developers and managers to edit the information concerned.

Personally, I would predict that any organisation currently implementing this formal structure would gradually devolve the editing remit from the developer role to the information owner. The intuitive nature of today's HTML authoring software is in many ways easier to use than word-processing software and can only help avoid occurrences of local Intranet developer 'bottleneck' arising.

Intranet management structures, example 2.

Alec Bruty, Intranet Development Manager at London Underground suggests a more formal Intranet Management Structure should be adopted (Bruty, 2000).

Figure 6. A sample organisational structure for managing Intranet publishing

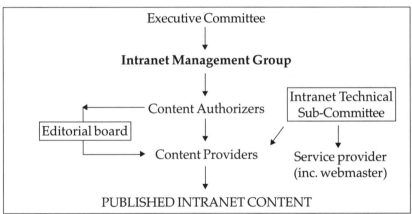

As can be seen in figure 6, one proposed method of managing an organisation's Intranet is to create an Intranet Management Structure comprising of the following components:

- Intranet Management Group
- Content authorisers
- Content providers
- Editorial board
- Service provider
- Intranet Technical Sub-Committee

Intranet Management Group (IMG)

The IMG is responsible for the strategic development and overall management of an organisation's Intranet. Reporting directly to the Executive Committee or Board, the remit of the group is to oversee any Service Level Agreements made between the parties that make up the structure, appoint Content Authorisers and review any decisions and recommendations made by the Intranet Technical Committee.

Content authorisers

Each major business area will have a Content authoriser who is then responsible for issuing licences to individuals to publish specific information. Bruty does however acknowledge that there may sometimes be a need for a Content authoriser's responsibility to span several business areas, to ensure that content of a common nature is not needlessly duplicated across the organisation. For instance, Health and Safety policies may be the same across the organisation, so it would make sense to have only one Content Authoriser issuing licences to publish this information rather than several Authorisers across the organisation issuing licences to several content providers who would then publish the same information.

Content Providers

The content provider is charged with similar duties as delegated to the role of Information Owner in the previous Intranet Management model. Whilst they are responsible for publishing information that fits the description of the licence issued to them by the Content Authoriser, they may still delegate the actual conversion process or 'button-pushing' to others. However the responsibility for ensuring that the information is maintained and the format ties in with agreed standards still lies with the Content Provider.

Editorial board

Editorial boards are set up at the discretion of the Content Authoriser to police both the format and content published by the Content Provider. An additional remit can also be to advise and provide information regarding other related sources that may be useful to include in the content under examination. Presumably then the members of these boards will need the same organisational or business overview as held by the Content authoriser. Maybe the most appropriate individuals to be members of the board would be Content Authorisers.

Service provider

The Service Provider is essentially responsible for ensuring that the technology underpinning the Intranet environment runs smoothly and the software that makes up all the 'bells and whistles' seen by the end-user are working correctly. The Service Level Agreement may also include software support for all users of Intranet related software across the Intranet Management Structure. This may not necessarily include the hardware such as the servers, the network operating system or network infrastructure. In terms of organisational roles close parallels can be drawn with that of the webmaster and Intranet team as described in the previous Intranet management model.

Intranet Technical Sub-Committee

Made up of representatives from the Intranet Management Group, Content Authorisers, Content Providers, Service Provider and IT department.

At the end of the day these structures are only models. Use of either of these models will depend on the existing structure and culture of your organisation. A combination of both might suit your current organisational structure.

Whatever structure is adopted, provision should also be made to allow an organisation to anticipate and plan how the organisation and dissemination of the corporate memory is managed. Whether it is the Intranet Team in the first model, or the Intranet Technical Sub-Committee in the second, which is charged with this remit, some kind of entity should be responsible for monitoring technological advancements and studies in the latest thoughts of knowledge creation and dissemination. With its unique ability to cascade information down through the organisation in an existing structure, this body can help an organisation evolve naturally by allowing all parts of the business to adapt naturally and at a realistic speed rather than having to react to ideas introduced through a big-bang approach. Constant cascading of such good practice through Intranet management structures will hopefully gain the support and confidence of the business as a whole and avoid an impression being created that such structures are bureaucratic and inflexible policy machines.

11.2 Electronic Document Management Systems

If the manual maintenance of information starts to become a problem for those originally charged with its management, then there may be a business case to support the purchase of an Electronic Document Management System (DMS). DMSs were around long before the advent of the WWW and have been most commonly used in large corporate departments responsible for the creation and maintenance of manuals, reports, product specifications, marketing literature and related records. Today's DMS have been further refined to help manage the additional complexities associated with web pages, namely the creation and maintenance of document hypertext links.

If your organisation is considering purchasing such a file management system, you may wish to evaluate whether it meets the following criteria as recommended by the Complete Intranet Resource (2000):

- Version control facility
- Ability to store metadata
- Security
- Check-in/check-out facility
- Search and indexing capability
- File interdependencies and groupings utilities
- Interface (open standard solution preferred where no client-side installs needed)
- Structure and organisational capabilities
- Supports multiple file types
- Maintain file expiration dates

The following sub-sections discuss some of the above issues that may need detailed consideration when selecting or developing your organisation's DMS.

Version control

Version control facilities allow details of editions to be recorded providing information of the author who made the changes, at what time and on which date. An example where this may be important is to allow previous versions to be maintained and labelled as a 'superseded' document, but still provide a means of using the information for reference purposes if there are any disputes or queries as to the original contents etc. Such control is often required as a compliance activity by organisations and may be a factor that is audited on an ongoing basis for accreditation by professional standards bodies or even a prominent customer requiring such quality assurances amongst their suppliers for audit trail purposes.

Storage of metadata

Metadata is data about data. In the case of document or file management... 'It describes the attributes and contents of an original document or work' (Milstead and Feldman, 1999). This may include information such as the author(s), the department, summaries and abstracts, keywords or thesauri describing the document or file content, the time and date of its creation, length, size, and the number of times the document has been edited.

Search engines are often text-based, so those files such as audio, video and graphics files can only be retrieved if accurate and relevant metadata are available describing the contents of the media or file. Text-based files also require metadata (bibliographic information) especially if the document is a lengthy one, as the search engine may not always be sophisticated enough to determine the subject matter through the indexing of the keywords contained in the document alone.

Security

Security is obviously of primary concern to any organisation that wishes to protect its intellectual property or knowledge-base. To ensure that an organisation can maximise this resource effectively, a document management system should have the controls in place to grant the appropriate networked access rights to its employees or even external third parties such as customers and suppliers. The security system should allow policies or rules to be easily applied to documents, as to who can read or not read a document, and who can edit or delete a document. These rules may even extend to the need to allow people to append a document with notifications of changes to information within the document or to add comments without having the authority to delete or change the original text.

Check-in/check-out facility

In a large organisation or even a small business where certain information will be accessed on a regular basis, scenarios can often arise where information accessed for reference purposes is also being simultaneously edited by others. Depending on the importance of this information, you may require your system to be able to do the following:

- block any kind of access to the document during the period it is being edited (whilst informing potential users of its current status regarding accessibility); you may also wish to inform any individuals as to who the current author is, in case there is any need to access this information urgently

- allow access to potential users but warn them that it is currently being amended

- allow editorial rights to different sections of a document according to a user's access rights – this has significant importance where a project team may be working on a report or documentation simultaneously

Search and indexing

There is little point in producing endless amounts of knowledge-based resources if authorised users cannot gain access to it. This is not just a case of ensuring that they have 'read-rights' to information, but to ensure that they can find it in the first place. Therefore search and indexing facilities are an essential part of any document management system. When drawing up your checklist of needs demanded of a potential DMS you may wish to investigate some of the following issues in more detail:

- are there cross-referencing facilities to related documents?
- does it integrate with existing search and indexing software in the organisation?
- does it allow free-text searching of the whole file or just the first few lines of the document?
- does the indexing facility include a controlled or uncontrolled thesaurus? Do you require both? Is there an automatic indexing facility?

Finally, one of the most important aspects relating to search facilities is the user-interface and the options presented to the user to search the resource. Some of your users may be experienced information professionals with a need for a system to meet sophisticated search criteria, whilst others will have a deep knowledge of the subject matter they are seeking but little experience in using such technology. The ability and flexibility of the search facilities adequately to meet these needs should be taken into account at the very beginning. A system that is not able to meet the search needs of the majority will tend to go unused. As this facility is often the main gateway facility used to access the information, an organisation's knowledge-base may go untapped if this need is not evaluated properly. More information is provided on the section referring to search engines.

File interdependencies and groupings utilities

In a typical organisation, information relating to the same subject, department or project will be held in a variety of electronic formats. For this reason any file management system should be capable of managing and grouping file formats that may range from office formats such as word-processed files and spreadsheets, to multimedia (including video, audio and graphics etc.).

Open standard interfaces

Again, referring to the theme of this book, it is obvious that a web-based interface would be advocated. Software is often described as platform independent in that it can be accessed via any web browser installed on any operating system. But is a web browser all that is required for a user to use the system? Be aware of any 'plug-ins' that may be required for the browser or additional ancillary files needed to be first installed on a given workstation. The need for such preparatory configurations can incur significant and costly overheads even if the process is a one-off. Just as important, the requirement of such client-side installs may raise significant barriers to accessing information, especially if access is to be provided for suppliers or customers where the host organisation has no control over these remote workstations or networks.

Structure and organisational capabilities

Just as operating system file storage structures can be copied, rearranged and moved, the same flexibility may also be required of a document management system. As departments or individual remits merge or expand and organisations merge with others, it is quite reasonable that file structures may need to change to reflect these developments. It is useful then to consider how flexible these systems would be in any proposed DMS.

Supports multiple file types

For an organisation truly to capitalise on all of the captured knowledge that is circulating, not only on the confines of the organisational Intranet but also the Internet, a document management system must allow its users to upload and download a wide variety of file formats. These include not just office suite formats such as wordprocessed files, spreadsheets, PowerPoint and database files but also jpeg, gif, audio and video (mpeg, avi, QuickTime, Real etc), HTML and pdf file formats.

Maintain file expiration dates

Many files or contents in an organisation have a limited lifespan. Examples may include conferences and corporate events, diary dates, job adverts, new library acquisitions, new staff appointments; and even canteen menus! At best some outdated information may just be seen as adding more irrelevant information for users to wade through in order to find what they want. At worst it may be inaccurate business-critical data such as price information or stock market data upon which someone makes an important decision. These problems can be alleviated, on the whole, by being given a predetermined date that the system recognises and deletes the information, thereby saving an individual having to spend valuable time in manually carrying out the task, and removing the opportunity for human error to occur. Some systems may even throw up a flag at predetermined times and dates to prompt administrators to check the validity of business-critical data to ensure that information that does not necessarily have a set life-span can still be inspected for its relevance at set intervals.

Document Management Systems are not new. Armed with this knowledge, potential purchasers should take this into consideration when evaluating products. Do they really allow the effective management of all forms of web content or are they just one of many revamped document management software products with a web front-end?

One management issue critical to the effective management of any web-based content relates to the use of hypertext links or hyperlinks. A dedicated content management system worth its salt will provide facilities for link creation and reporting faulty or dead links.

Cisco also warns against some inconsistent features to be aware of when choosing such a product (Whitlock, 2000). In a white paper discussing such issues relating to Content management software, products are highlighted that allow all links to be checked across a site at the click of a button. Yet, if a file name or location is changed the system does not automatically update all the links to this resource at the same time. This process, also known as link management, can be critical in retaining user confidence in the Intranet. Such an automated system can pay for itself in a short space of time due to the significant amount of human intervention that would otherwise be required to rectify the faults.

Email notification systems may also be an additional facility required by users who may hold remits in specific workflow processes or editorial roles and only access documents periodically or as a one-off procedure. In this case, email notification can alert this infrequent user automatically when a document is edited, reaches a certain stage of the workflow process or is ready for authorisation to be published onto the Intranet.

There has however been research that suggests implementing such systems is not all plain sailing. Problems fall into two main areas and both relate to high start-up costs. Forrester Research (Waltner, 1999) carried out one such study into the issues surrounding the management of Intranet content and highlighted that the steep learning curve required in implementing these solutions typically can require months rather than weeks of staff time to be invested in bringing the system on-line. Start-up costs for the software alone can typically be upwards of $50,000.

Figure 7. Comparative costs for several leading Document Management Systems.

Product:	Livelink by Open Text (http://www.opentext.com)
Price:	$125,000 for 100 user/contributor seats including server licence; additional contributor seats $97
Product:	Ncompass by Ncompass Labs (http://www.ncompasslabs.com)
Price:	$39,000 per server, 10 author seats and 2 designer seat licences
Product:	Participant Server Eprise (http://www.eprise.com)

Price: $50,000 per server

Product: TeamSite by Interwoven (www.interwoven.com)

Price: $70,000 per server licence and 10 user/contributor licences

Due to the substantial numbers of documents and content required to be held by these systems, powerful databases often sit at the back-end of the software. It is wise therefore to establish at the beginning whether these systems include their own integrated database management system or whether an Oracle or SQL system is also required as an additional overhead.

One company which has recently implemented a web content management application is the Tandy Corporation (PR Newswire, 2000). Tandy has selected FileNET's Panagon Web Services as a foundation for the company's Intranet content management solution. By the end of 2001, it is expected that as many as 5,000 of the company's RadioShack stores will be connected to the new Intranet. It is claimed that personnel in each store will be able to access business-critical information necessary for the running of daily operations. Information will include policies and procedures, corporate directories and contacts, product repair manuals, point of sale manuals, and promotional and sales incentive programmes; information that up until now has only been available from the store point-of-sale system or by snail-mail from company headquarters.

11.3 Content management and extranets

The content management principles and tools discussed so far are often identical to those applied when managing the content of an extranet. Just as an Intranet holds the potential for making significant savings by maintaining a single source of information as opposed to several hard copy versions, this principle can be capitalised on further by utilising the same content for use in both Intranet and extranet services.

Access privileges for static HTML web pages by the various user groups accessing extranet services is easy enough to implement, especially by using the methods already mentioned. However, restricting access to certain data or information contained within these documents for some users, whilst allowing others different levels of access, is more problematic.

To avoid having to reproduce versions containing varying degrees of detail for different users, a more effective method of managing this information is to segment it across several database fields. The data is always current and different user groups can be permitted access to preconfigured levels of detail and data fields without any additional human intervention once the original data has been entered.

Kurt Christopherson, UK e-business development manager for 3Com, re-iterates the importance of these issues when developing an extranet:

> 'The same single source database should feed both the Intranet and extranet electronically without re-entering, or time-delaying the data. Not only should there be a single database, but also just one person or department responsible for each type of source information – such as pricing – to avoid inconsistencies and duplication of effort.'

(Hunter, 1999)

Practical examples where this method of information and data management might be applied could include:

- personnel records containing employee details such as home address and salary etc., that are accessible to their respective line manager via the Intranet, whilst their 'name, job title, email and telephone extension numbers' are the only data fields that are accessible to customers and suppliers via the extranet.
- product data records that allow sales personnel to view the fields detailing the corporate approved minimum sales/profit margins, whilst customers or business partners see the field detailing the standard retail price.

Organisations which may not yet be in a position to develop both Intranet and extranet services may be persuaded to opt for the cheaper storage method of holding information in static HTML web pages. Although this may be the least costly method initially, it is likely to prove the more expensive option in the long run if the information is required to be segmented into database fields, especially as existing and prospective extranet users demand increasing amounts of functionality in the future.

Some general tips then for managing extranet content might include:

- 'publish just once or be damned' – do not establish separate databases for the extranet. Create single sources of information
- Establish well-defined points of ownership: give individuals or small groups the specific responsibility for each of the data sources, avoiding inconsistency and redundant effort
- Use the Intranet as a test-bed for extranet services to test security and privileged levels of access
- Carefully assess the value of all information you intend to publish or make available via the extranet
- Once you know the value of the information to be published, decide how much security you need to protect it

- Segment the information to be published as far as possible so that multiple logical extranets can be created to serve different categories of user.

- Create user profiles defining the kind of information they need and the order with which it should be presented within their web site. The ultimate aim is to give every user a personal, virtual extranet.

- Implement management tools to track the course of transactions across an extranet and to identify bottlenecks

(Hunter, 1999)

Chapter 12

Enhancing web content

As mentioned in Part II of the book, one of the easiest methods of filling the Intranet is to convert existing documentation and information already in electronic format. This is fine as a policy to ensure that there is content for your users to retrieve in the first place, but as time moves on users are unlikely to return to this information if it is not maintained, developed, and relevant information is not easily extracted. Internet Design Magazine provides 'Eight practical tips for creating high-impact web content' (Anton, 2000) that can help encourage users to return to useful information and enable their participation and feeling of joint ownership in developing content. These guidelines have been adapted and expanded upon below:

1. 'Present instructional content in small chunks or "sound bites" so that information can be easily digested and remembered'

There will be a large percentage of instructional type material placed on your Intranet, whether these are Service Level Agreements for customers and suppliers or instructions on how to access the voice mail system. Users will not find it easy to read a solid page of Times New Roman text in font size 10. Authors should take advantage of the use of colours, 'white space', and headings that the HTML format provides which will help users better to digest and memorise information. However, do avoid going overboard with decorated images that provide no additional and salient information. Pages are no longer restrained in having to be strictly A4 in length, so take advantage of adding extra text to content where you might have ordinarily tried to conserve space so that everything fitted neatly onto a double-sided handout.

Another thing not to be tempted into, is to use the full space provided by the width of a standard workstation monitor. The reason for the popularity of a standard book or novel size is not just because it is convenient for travelling, or for carrying in pockets. A typical novel or newspaper column is easy to read because it only requires the reader's eyes to move and not the head. This may not sound such a grave issue when reading a paragraph or two from the left-hand side of a screen to the right, but consider how annoying this will become for the reader when they are required to read a whole manual or report in this manner.

2.   'Meet the needs of multiple audiences'

Different employees with different job functions and in different departments will have varying interests in any information on the Intranet.
Department heads may just need an overview of the subject matter whilst
technicians and engineers require more detailed information. Hyperlinked
contents pages and summaries will help accommodate many of these
different levels of interest, as will links to more complex graphics.

The above issues have only focused on the needs of employees from the
perspective of occupational remits. Equally as important and relating
especially to UK legislature is ensuring all employees have equal access
to information regardless of the physical ability of the individual.

3.   'Build in hot-links and cross-references to related information'

Provide hyperlinks to other information that may be of interest. Information relating to the author's broad interests, job function or areas of
expertise is an additional way of promoting valuable networks and knowledge creation in the organisation.

4.   'Web documents should promote two-way, interactive communi-
        cation between the author and the reader so that the readers can
        quickly give their feedback'

Regardless of the quality checks in place to ensure data and information
is correct before it is published on an Intranet, mistakes will always occur
whether they are a result of human error, information becoming outdated
or links to other resources becoming obsolete. One way to guard against
this information remaining incorrect for longer periods than necessary is
to provide a mechanism for feedback from the reader back to the author. It
is therefore important to include at least an email address for the author.

Feedback facilities are not only useful for the purpose of informing authors of mistakes. From a knowledge management perspective, automated
feedback forms can provide readers with the opportunity to add more
value to existing published knowledge. This can include the posting of
other related sites of interest. You may also want to gauge the value that
users place on the document. Log files can provide limited automatically
generated information, such as the number of times a page has been
accessed, but only the use of web forms and check boxes can allow a
reader to provide qualitative information relating to how useful or not
they found the document to be.

Links can be made to forums (virtual discussion areas) for the express
purpose of discussing salient issues further and allow employees to share
their expertise or ask for advice relating to the original subject matter of
the document.

5. 'Provide media options to meet the learning and comprehension needs of a vast audience'

Try to take advantage of the multimedia formats that can be offered over the Intranet. Instructional type information may benefit significantly from the use of video clips or a diagram to demonstrate a point or task.

6. 'Do not force the reader to scroll through the entire document'

One of the many traps that authors can fall into when converting native word-processed files into HTML (especially with newsletters etc.) is to maintain twin column formats. This may work fine in hard copy formats but can be disorientating if not plain irritating if the reader has continuously to scroll up and down the screen to read the next line of a paragraph. The regular use of 'anchors' or hyperlinks back to the contents page or related sections elsewhere in the document will help improve the navigation of documents for the reader, especially if they stretch to several pages in length.

Chapter 13

Implementing a publishing policy

Encouraging the adoption of such best practice is often achieved through establishing an organisation-wide publishing policy. Providing templates and guidelines for authors to adhere to, when publishing content on the Intranet, can help dramatically to improve the appearance of the Intranet, whilst also speeding up the process of generating the content itself. Specific advantages of introducing publishing policies, in addition to those already mentioned in the previous chapter may include:

- people have more faith in something that looks official and in the corporate format

- help ensure that the content can be read by all different types of browsers

- if at some stage the content is to be transferred to the Internet or be made available to customers, time will not be needlessly wasted in reformatting the document for wider consumption

- if the Intranet provides access to sister businesses, access to external sites or purchased content, orientation on the part of the user will be significantly improved if the document is readily identified as originating from the parent organisation.

When the Research Library and Information Services at Ford Motor Company recently attempted the transition from traditional publishing methods to one that was web-based they found that authors of their technical reports resisted the change and voiced the following common complaints:

> 'Some authors do not like their work published on the Web because of presentation difficulties—HTML is not an elegant format for reading on-screen, and many graphs, charts, and other images lose some definition (compared to photographs) when converted into GIF or JPEG (or even Adobe PDF) formats.'

> (Primich and Varnum, 1999).

With training and advice, backed up with frequently updated publishing policies, the organisation can help dispel this kind of resistance and help content providers to avoid some of the pitfalls they may well experience if they are otherwise left to their own devices.

Chapter 14

Information overload

Information overload occurs when the amount of time required to read and process incoming information exceeds the amount of time available to the individual for this purpose. Business correspondence, junk-mail, telephone calls, meetings, memos, faxes, newsletters and ad hoc conversations on the way to the vending machine, have always been plentiful in keeping the average worker occupied (or distracted?) even before the advent of Internet technologies in the workplace. If it was a straightforward case of these new technologies replacing their conventional counterparts then the results of this transition may not prove to be such a problem. Unfortunately, like most changes in work-processes, there is an extended period of transition as the new process becomes the norm. In the meantime, until the ubiquitous virtual and paper-less office arrives, this new influx of information is added to the existing forms of information coming into our working environment.

Despite these issues regarding workload it is easy to see why people have readily accepted the technology. Email has revolutionised the way employees can now communicate, enabling them to work flexibly, communicate and gain access to customers, suppliers and fellow employees alike. The way in which email can transcend bureaucratic and hierarchical structures in an organisation to speed up business processes lends itself well to the flatter and more organically structured organisation that has been emerging over recent years.

A report by Ferris Research (2000) entitled, *Quantifying the Productivity Gains of Email* claims that productivity gains of 15 percent are achievable through the use of email over traditional forms of office communication.

> 'Faster business cycles and improved decision-making are important benefits to an email-based office that are not readily quantifiable', suggests David Ferris, president of Ferris Research and further comments. 'If you ignore the intangible benefits and focus on the quantifiable benefits alone, such as time saved compared to processing faxes, filing documents, and playing telephone tag, you can document that email introduces clear, substantial cash savings'.

The study, based on information from 29 organisations, claims that gains for the average office user due to the use of email are 381 hours or $12,919 annually. However there now appears to be a plateau where this productivity peaks. If the influx of this information is not kept in check productivity can quickly nosedive as it takes a psychological hold on office workers. The Ferris Research estimates that losses incurred as a result of email use are 115 hours or $3919 annually.

The ease with which vast amounts of information can now come flooding onto the desktop can have a serious detrimental effect on the organisation and employee in two ways:

a)   firstly, the productivity of the employee can be dramatically affected because of the nature in which digital information distracts the individual from doing their core job function and more importantly;

b)   the stressful nature of trying then to catch up with their day-to-day critical remit can have a very serious effect on the health of the employee

Reuters, the news agency, claim in their 'guide to good information strategy' that:

'In the UK alone, information overload contributes up to 30m working days a year lost through stress-related illnesses at a cost of some £2 billion.'

(Reuters, 2000)

The guide also claims that constant exposure to information overload leads to a condition termed Information Fatigue Syndrome (IFS) which can often be observed in the form of the following symptoms:

• an inability to make decisions or cope in other ways
• irritability and anger
• pain in the stomach and muscles
• frequent feelings of helplessness, listlessness and lethargy
• inability to sleep at night, waking in the small hours with a sense of panic
• loss of energy and enthusiasm for hobbies or leisure activities

The average amount of time that users spent dealing with their electronic correspondence two years ago was approximately 90 minutes per day. A recent survey by 'The User Group' (Guardian, 2000) claims this has risen to almost three hours a day and if left unchecked could rise to four hours a day. The survey highlights that the bulk of the problem comes not from junk-mail or 'spam' but is created by employees in the organisation. It is thought that this apparent fury of activity has little to do with conscientious workers nurturing a well-informed community but purely a form of electronic politics with originators of emails sending copies to people in order to 'cover their backs' or impress managers who do not need to read them. This then creates even more never ending 'loops' of token comments in an attempt to display equal or competing levels of dedication. Meanwhile, the unwitting manager is forced to observe a game of email-tennis.

The survey by The User Group identifies the following problematic areas associated with overload and ranked in the following order:

- Copied mail   30%
- Junk mail   24%
- Internal lists   18%
- No training   16%
- Private mail   12%

    (Business & Technology, 2000)

Unfortunately, this kind of counterproductive use of the technology is unlike junk-mail in the sense that 'spam' can be filtered straight into the 'recycling' bin. Putting such blocks on correspondence from your work colleagues however is fraught with danger. It is likely that sooner or later a critical piece of information will be missed and not acted upon.

Another form of email misuse, but this time far more innocently intended, is received from the 'virus warning do-gooder'.

The 'virus warning do-gooder' phenomenon is an issue that is worth raising here especially as organisations often turn a blind eye to the problem. Yet, this is a problem that can cost more in resource terms than the very same security breach about which the 'forwarder' of the email is trying to warn you. What are they trying to warn you about? More often than not, it is a hoax virus to which they refer. The hoax virus can quite easily be more prolific than a genuine virus. Why?

a)   any prankster can write a virus warning – no programming skills are needed - only an ability to type!;

b)   well-meaning friends, relatives and colleagues new to Internet technology are only too happy to spread the warning on to others

If you ever received a hoax virus-warning take a look at the 'cc:' list if you have not done so already. Even if you refrain from passing on this message it is likely a significant number in this list have already passed the message on again, only this time to another dozen friends, colleagues and relatives in their address book. This pyramid networking effect can often use up valuable resources as these messages do the rounds. Here, an effective information security policy can alleviate this problem through educating users. Although training individuals to recognise potential hoaxes or compare them to a list of known hoaxes held on the Intranet may be a little ambitious, merely educating the user to forward the warning to the IT department will help significantly reduce the negative effect this phenomenon has on the organisation.

So how can these problems be abated?

Below are some tips or methods for alleviating information overload on the Intranet and some useful measures that may be employed in any related educational or training provision.

Email filters

Most email software packages allow the user to filter or 'screen' messages based on a number of criteria. Based on author, subject, size or whether they have attachments etc., messages can be filtered into specific directories, forwarded on to relevant people or deleted. This is specifically useful if you subscribe to any newsletters or mailing lists that do not require your immediate attention, allowing them to be automatically steered into dedicated folders for you to read at a more convenient time. The use of this system can almost be seen as an automatic document control or management system allowing the user not just to get a clearer picture of what reading should be given priority, but also provides a means of easily finding the information at a later date.

Other related uses include:

- Setting rules for personal messages to be filtered into separate folders
- Filtering messages from your boss

Many mailing lists now have protocols for the syntax used in subject headings so as to allow users quickly to identify what is and is not relevant to themselves as they appear in their respective 'in-trays'. These may include 'conference notices' or 'job vacancies' that can therefore be deleted instantly or diverted into specific folders. Try to encourage your work colleagues to adopt similar practices - this practice is especially useful for saving time in organising similar documentation relating to projects etc.

Rerouting 'spam'

Spam is the electronic equivalent of junk mail and is so common that it is generally accepted as an occupational hazard these days. However, there are measures to guard against this problem turning from an occasional nuisance to becoming a frustrating and time-consuming pastime, trying to sift through what is junk and what is business related. Things to be wary of that might increase junk-mail from a trickle to a flood are:

- Volunteering your email address to a commercial or shopping site asking to be kept informed of special offers

- Subscribing to free newsletters or journals (either on-line or in print-form) and providing your email address; take note of the disclaimers at the bottom of these 'sign-up' sheets - invariably there are always 'tick boxes' asking you if you would wish to have your details forwarded to third parties or not!

If you are continuously receiving unsolicited email from a known source, simply set up a filter to direct the message straight into the recycle bin. However, if you are receiving multiple occurrences of messages with the same subject, but from a range of spurious sources, set the filter to trash anything with that particular heading i.e. 'Get a free degree today' or 'Your loan has just been approved' which are just a sample of unsolicited messages that constantly do the rounds.

Unsubscribe to services and updates

One of the consequences of email is the way in which it is all too easy to see a newsletter, think that it may be interesting, subscribe and then find a few weeks or months down the line that you are receiving six similar newsletters or electronic alert bulletins - none of which you have the time to read! It would be fine if we all had time to read this information but, think realistically, do you really need this information?

Likewise think about mailing lists as well. Is there really enough useful information that you are receiving via this service to warrant checking through the whole contents?

It could very well be the case however that once in a while, useful or critical information is provided in these sources. If there are particular services that are of general interest to everyone in your section or department is it possible to nominate specific individuals in your section to subscribe to these items and then forward any relevant information to others if it is relevant?

Things to watch out for before you send

Check the CC: list. Is it necessary to email all the people listed? Even if you think there is some Machiavellian benefit from ensuring that every manager up to Chief Executive status sees what a wonderful hardworking and conscientious individual you are, personal email policies such as this can soon backfire. It is just as likely that these emails will irritate the very same people you are trying to impress and every chance that you will receive several token replies that you really do not need to spend time perusing.

Try also to refrain from forwarding chain letters, jokes and urban legends.

If you are about to send an email with a file attachment, is it really necessary? Attachments can rapidly use up memory space allocations, both in your sent directory and the in-box of your recipient's in-box. Publish it on the Intranet if it isn't there already and provide the URL for it. This is also good document management practice as the file your recipients will be accessing will always be the most current.

Ignace Direckens, the ICT Manager for VDAB (the Flemish Service for Employment Consultancy and Vocational Training) acknowledged (Chapman, 1999) that this was a problem in their own organisation when their groupware system became too popular. As a result of its impact everyone started to email documents to each other causing bandwidth, document control and overload problems. The solution for the organisation was to place all central policies and procedures on a central Intranet to allow people the option to decide when and whether this information was relevant to them.

This is also especially considerate in respect of remote workers who may otherwise have to download several large files over a slow modem connection. This policy will enable them to download files at their own convenience and give them the choice of determining whether the files are of interest.

Check your email periodically instead of becoming a slave to the alert 'chime' for new mail. Often so-called urgent emails and related issues resolve themselves in the interim.

Training

The points covered so far may go a long way to helping alleviate information overload problems at both an individual level and organisation-wide level especially if seen to be sanctioned by the organisation. Such approval by the organisation would be both visible and extremely useful in its own right if these issues and recommendations are provided in relevant training and induction sessions.

These measures become even more effective when they are adopted as corporate-wide policy. The Ferris Research report (Ferris Research, 2000) shows that companies, which encourage employees to limit the personal use of email, shorten distribution lists and reduce indiscriminate copying, can achieve measurable increases in productivity rather than declines. The report claims that the productivity gains of 15 percent mentioned earlier in the section can reach 20 percent if management takes simple steps to train workers in effective use of email, including setting policies and culture to discourage personal use and excessive distribution.

It should be noted that this information overload might not just arise through information 'pushed' at the individual through such technologies as email. It can also be partly self-imposed at any time when the employee is trying to retrieve or pull information from a sea of other irrelevant information.

Careful use of the World Wide Web and refining of search and retrieval strategies can also go a long way to helping alleviate personal information overload.

Selective browsing

Ensure your bookmarks are well organised. Spend five or ten minutes creating folders for your bookmarks. Don't convince yourself that you will do it later. This small investment in spending your time organising your bookmarks can pay dividends in the long run, enabling you quickly to find them in the future, and prevents the need to research and re-bookmark the locations of interesting sites.

Save time by refining your search criteria when using search engines. Whether you are using search engines on your Intranet or on the Internet, ten minutes spent reading the help files provided with search engines will save you hours of searching in the long run.

Despite the access to the Internet becoming ever more accessible in even the least technologically advanced countries in the world, the USA is still the world's principal user of the Internet. With the East Coast five hours behind GMT and the West Coast eight hours behind, access speeds to the Internet in Europe slow down dramatically from 1pm in the afternoon onwards. This may sound obvious to seasoned surfers but will come as a revelation to some new graduates or staff previously denied access to the Internet, and should therefore be part of any induction and educational programme.

Unified messaging (UM) also offers a means of alleviating information overload problems. UM provides a standard Graphical User Interface to all forms of digital communication including fax, voicemail and email. However such claims are still relatively unfounded as yet due to the limited number of vendors and their recent arrival on the market, which leaves the technology relatively unproven.

Part IV

Integration

Chapter 15

Integrating knowledge management with your Intranet strategy

Stage 4: integration

This is a point in time where the controls and procedures are now embedded within the quality assurance systems and culture of the organisation. The Intranet becomes the 'definitive record' of all information, process, knowledge and therefore learning that exists in the organisation.

This stage represents the required threshold of the Intranet's evolution from that of the organisation's central information repository to becoming the 'corporate memory' (Kuhn and Abecker, 1999). The prevailing issue now is the continuous improvement of processes that nurture the capture, sharing and creation of knowledge.

Once the Intranet's ability to add real value to a business as an effective information and communication system had been recognised, so it quickly became apparent that this was a tool with the potential for being the key enabling factor to delivering an organisation's Knowledge Management strategy.

It should be realised though, that an enabling tool is all an Intranet can be at this stage. The existence of email clients, web browsers and any amount of static content cannot on its own exploit the benefits of Knowledge Management (KM). However, there are some managers and authors (Mattinson, 1999) who would argue that the recording and making explicit of expertise and knowledge as static content is, in itself, a knowledge management process.

Some quarters may hold the view that knowledge may simply be harvested and held as static content and that it is purely technology-led, whilst others may claim that it is a cultural and people-centric issue, which will determine whether any KM strategy will succeed or fail (Hendriks and Vriens, 1999).

Knowledge Management: the definition

Where both extremes of these perspectives do agree is in the acknowledgement that a KM strategy is worth pursuing. So what is it exactly?

KM has been around as a concept for a long time. Part of the reason for KM enjoying such a renaissance can be attributed largely to the advent of the Intranet as a complementary enabling technology. This is certainly a view held by Ovum, the independent research consultancy, which suggests in a recent report that 'Intranets have been used by many user organisations to challenge and bypass existing barriers to communication', and '...forced organisations to think through their information content strategy, from the capture of ideas to the structure of data, and the storage and distribution of knowledge'. (Ovum, 1999).

For a more definitive explanation of what KM is, we first need to define knowledge. Knowledge is generally recognised to exist in two forms, namely 'explicit' knowledge and 'tacit' knowledge.

Explicit knowledge is tangible information and is readily available for dissemination, scrutiny and examination by others. This knowledge may take the form of memos, emails, reports and other documented materials whereas tacit knowledge is not so readily available for capture and dissemination. Tacit knowledge is the knowledge held within us, combined with personal perspectives, experience, emotional intelligence and 'gutfeelings'. This is essentially the intellectual capital of an organisation.

It is the process of capturing and sharing both these types of knowledge and their use in creating new knowledge with which Knowledge Management is principally concerned.

The use of technology to disseminate explicit knowledge is fairly transparent. This is especially so when this documented knowledge is available for storage and retrieval on the organisation-wide Intranet and is obviously a product-centred view of knowledge management.

However, the use of technology to make tacit knowledge more readily available to share can be considered more of a challenge for an organisation and the knowledge manager. This process-centred management of knowledge uses technology to enable the social communication processes that exist when two or more people collaborate and work together. This process is known as Computer Supported Collaborative Working (CSCW) and utilises software known as groupware or Group Support Systems (GSS) (Dhaliwal and Tung, 2000). This enables people to work on-line and create new knowledge. As work, discussions and projects progress, the group-decision processes and any related documents appear as transcripts now digitised and available for re-use by anyone permitted access to this virtual workspace (or the archive if the discourse and work is now complete).

Systems can be built into CSCW to allow others to add comments or 'signposts' to related information and knowledge. This will further enhance the Intranet's ability to share and nurture the creation of new knowledge across the organisation.

The application of a systems approach alone to KM is doomed to failure. A significant reason for this lies in the fact that it is highly unlikely that employees are going to welcome a tool or philosophy that appears to have the sole intention of capturing their valuable and hard-earned expertise and subsequently threaten to make the individual appear surplus to requirements. Advocates for this approach often claim this is the way to ensure that an organisation's intellectual knowledge does not walk out of the door when a key member of the business resigns or retires or downsizing occurs.

On a more practical level, the reality of today's fast moving markets, changing technologies and consumer trends means that the life span of knowledge with true marketable value is limited. Even with a workforce committed to a systems approach, by the time this knowledge has been captured, assessed for its business value, and categorised ready for retrieval it has quickly become outdated. If 'knowledge workers' are not available to replenish, update and build upon this knowledge then it will quickly stagnate and become redundant. Therefore an organisation's knowledge-base should be able to encompass a constantly changing repository of information that both feeds 'knowledge workers' that is in turn fed back as newly created knowledge.

The purpose of the technology then, in this model, is not to serve as a static database but as a conduit to act as a catalyst for many-to-many communication. With such a commonly accessible interface as the Intranet web browser, the opportunity of implementation becomes more readily achievable.

Chapter 16

Groupware

What is Groupware?

Groupware is the term generally used to describe software packages that provide a collaborative work environment for use by employees. Either to allow group communication, decision-making, document sharing or generation, or to provide a means of allowing different parts of an organisation to work through a business process in a shared electronic environment, which would traditionally have been worked through using paper-based systems or face-to-face communications.

Two distinct forms of communication are usually in evidence in Groupware products. These are asynchronous and synchronous.

Asynchronous communication occurs when there is a time delay in the communication process and the individuals or groups involved are unable to give a real-time (i.e. immediate) response to the sender of the message or information.

Examples include email, voicemail, fax, electronic and physical bulletin/notice boards, and post-it notes.

The opposite of 'asynchronous' communication then, is 'synchronous' communication. In contrast, this is a form of communication that permits and is designed to allow responses to be made in real-time, requiring the communicating parties to engaged in the process at the same time.

Examples include telephone conversations, video-conferencing, electronic 'chat', face-to-face meetings and 'white-boarding'.

Specific components of Groupware become ever more difficult to generalise as vendors add increasing numbers of value-added utilities or 'bells and whistles'. Typical components, depending on the product, may include:

- Email systems
- Group calendar systems (for either department team scheduling or project management purposes)
- Contacts databases

- Discussion boards or conferencing areas (asynchronous, synchronous) sometimes with white-boarding, voice, video as well as common text-based communication utilities
- Document management systems

From a business-process perspective there are three main applications that can be identified. Groupware can be used as a: shared reference library, Computer-Supported Collaborative Working (CSCW) systems and, Workflow Management Systems (WfMS). These variations of groupware are discussed further in the following sections.

16.1 Shared reference library

These are systems that provide access to shared documents. These may be technical reports, company price lists, annual reports, internal memoranda, or internally produced reference resources. Increasingly these areas will include more multimedia such as PowerPoint slides, audio and video presentations.

16.2 Computer-Supported Collaborative Working (CSCW) systems

This form of communication allows groups of workers to communicate as they would in face-to-face environments only (mostly) by text-based means. This allows workers, displaced by both time and geographical difference, to maintain dialogue whilst working on problems, projects or policy from their respective remote locations. Once a project team is dispersed, or at a predetermined milestone, this information can be approved for disseminating to a wider audience. The transcripts can then be archived for reference purposes so that the organisation as a whole can search this repository and benefit from gaining access to the expertise and learning contained within.

As far as the technology and social dynamics are concerned, Computer-Supported Collaborative Learning and CSCW environments are almost identical. Virtual or Managed Learning Environments are becoming increasingly common for delivering distance learning solutions for all enterprises, from both a practical point of view and from the perspective of improving the quality of the learning experience.

The benefits inherent in both CSCW and CSCL are that the asynchronous nature of the communication promotes reflection upon the subject matter or topic of discussion, thereby permitting deeper thought and more considered responses regarding the subject matter or problem in hand. The environment acts as a catalyst for true teamworking. This is helped in part by typical power-based relationships associated with face-to-face environments being marginalised or removed, factors that might otherwise interfere with effective groupwork. For instance, everyone in this kind of environment gets to have their say and no one is able to dominate proceedings. Time restrictions are also removed. So, whereas a typical meeting may be cut short due to time restrictions, this environment is not limited by such limitations. However, it should be realised that like all asynchronous forms of communication, decision-making can take longer than in a face-to-face meeting if approval is sought by all interested parties. Although this argument is negligible, if the parties are required to fly from different countries for such meetings.

Bell Atlantic has gone one step further in pursuing the goal of becoming a learning organisation (*see also* chapter – training and education) by combining their education programmes with their knowledge management systems. As opposed to the majority of web learning environments that centre on the virtual collaboration and co-operation of members of a specific class, Bell Atlantic's Knowledge Depot focuses on the organisation as a whole. Regardless of their location the system helps students bring their working context to the forum by allowing individuals to work in groups that share similar working practices and interests, rather than the binding factor being purely related to their location, same college or working hours. As is often realised with any Computer-Supported Collaborative Learning programme, Bell Atlantic claim:

> '…these conversations help surface tacit knowledge by allowing people to describe how to do a task, others are conversations in which members provide support to each other but do not necessarily share knowledge.'

(Zimmerman et al, 2000)

To enable the organisation to capitalise on these valuable knowledge repositories, the system was specifically designed so that the 'content' could be automatically structured or restructured at a later date. Search facilities are then provided to enable other employees to gain access to this knowledge.

Research has also strongly indicated (Blackmore, 2000) that this kind of environment provides participants with the opportunity to improve their overall generic and employability skills.

Some of the attributes that are observed to be acquired or refined include: group productivity; social and emotional competencies; memorisation and retrieval of information; competence in co-operative situations; cognitive development and related areas of social adjustment; communication effectiveness; autonomous moral judgement; empathetic ability; positive attitudes towards the subject in hand; reduction of prejudices and the appreciation of cultural and individual differences (especially useful in an organisation with a transnational Intranet!); development of positive self-attitudes and a belief in one's personal worth; an understanding and appreciation of motivational issues; development of interpersonal skills; behaviour based upon intrinsic motivation.

Similar research has provided evidence that the following traits are also nurtured in CSCL and CSCW environments:

- helps clarify ideas and concepts through discussion
- develops critical thinking
- provides opportunities for learners to share information and ideas
- develops communications skills
- provides a context where the learners can take control of their own learning in a social context
- provides validation of individuals' ideas and ways of thinking through conversation (verbalising); multiple perspectives (cognitive restructuring); and argument (conceptual conflict resolution)

    (McConnell, 1994)

Bell Atlantic also appears to have recognised the acquisition of skills inherent in such working and learning environments. In defining what was important to the business, beyond a traditional curriculum, the organisation defined a set of 'Umbrella Competencies' that would encourage '…behavioral, cultural, and organisational changes needed to help create a learning organisation'.

These skills, that are woven into each programme of study, focus upon quality, teamwork, teambuilding, leadership, technology, customer focus, interpersonal skills, and problem solving and instructing skills. A member of the Next Step Programme describes how the environment helps nurture these very same competencies desired by the organisation stating:

> 'A few databases and other physical resources would be practically useless without the camaraderie, teamwork and, yes, friendly competition fostered by the programme.'

British Telecom (Midwinter and Sheppard, 2000) has highlighted some less obvious benefits that can be reaped by organisations, using so-called e-Collaboration technology in general, relating to areas in:

- remote experts – the technology also provides the flexibility to allow 'remote experts' to be invited into a conference as necessary. Instead of having to put a decision off until the correct people can be invited to a follow-up meeting, they can be invited into a conference as the need for their expertise becomes clear, greatly reducing the decision-making period

- results-oriented meetings – the new technology is being seen to make meetings much more productive and results-oriented, with information available to all participants at once. This means that minutes, actions and results can be shared in real-time for immediate correction and agreement for action

- meeting culture is changing – meetings are becoming less formal, with team members being able to continue with their normal work in the background, while listening to a part of the meeting which is of less relevance to them, and then becoming fully active as the subject changes back to something more relevant

Purchasing issues

If you wish to utilise software specifically for meeting or conferencing functions you may want to consider purchasing software dedicated to meet this need. Examples of popular products in this market include:

Ultimate BB ~ http://www.ultimatebb.com
Ultra Board ~ http://www.ultraboard.org
WebBoard ~ http://webboard.oreilly.com

16.3 Workflow management systems

This is a process management system that allows a designated number of people, either in the same department, or across business functions, to process work activities collaboratively in a parallel and/or sequential manner. Due to the collaborative nature of the work processes that may be separated by both time and location it can be viewed as a form of CSCW as described above. The system aids the speedy sequential processing of documentation in which different individuals or departments are charged with the remit of approving or editing documents at any given stage. A basic workflow example may be:

Approval for the publication of reports, whereby the process may include: an author first submitting a technical report to the system; their line manager approving its relevance; suitability and quality of the content; the Library and Information Service or technical library appointing a report number and suitable keywords/taxonomy; and finally the line manager developing/approving a circulation list for appropriate distribution.

Similar processes may include the approval of expense claims, purchase orders or application for leave entitlement.

Definitions in the literature generally mirror the following:

'A workflow management system (WFMS) is a computer-based information system for the support of distributed work tasks in a company. The WFMS is based on control structures (i.e.

workflows), which are used for triggering, co-ordination and supervision of activities.'

(Dangelmaier et al., 1999)

The advent of Intranet and extranet platforms has dramatically increased the business value of workflow applications across an organisation. Using the Internet or Intranet removes any specialist knowledge in connecting to applications across multiple network configurations and allows workers seamlessly to access workflow systems at the click of a mouse via the web browser. Staff from all over the world in any time zone can now process workflows more quickly than any previously adopted site-based workflow solutions. This seamlessness connectivity can also be seen to help marginalise any issues surrounding operational disadvantages perceived to exist for the remote worker compared to the corporate site-based employee.

Through the Internet or extranet, mobile and teleworkers can be assigned their workload automatically and dynamically according to their respective job functions and working hours. Workloads and progress of each individual or groups can then be monitored by the relevant managers who may be based centrally or even remotely themselves (Workflow Management Coalition, 1998a).

Many similarities can be drawn between Workflow Management Systems and Content/Document Management Systems but this is mainly due to the fact that both systems ultimately manage recorded information at some point in the respective systems. The principal differences are that WFMSs are designed to facilitate collaborative work processes and therefore the nature of the information is often dynamic, whereas Content Management Systems are essentially concerned with its effective dissemination and maintenance; that on the whole means the information is in a static state. However, a Document Management System is often an essential component of any WFMS and may exist as either an integral element of the system or integrated as a bolt-on component in the form of a legacy system (Dangelmaier et al., 1999).

Many of these differences become more apparent when criteria are identified that can be used to compare and evaluate workflow systems. The following criteria can be used to evaluate both technological and organisational aspects of systems. Technological aspects include those that relate to the features and functionality of the software whilst the organisational aspects relate to issues surrounding implementation and operational management of the system (Perez and Rojas, 2000).

When determining which WFMS will best suit your organisation you may wish to consider some of the following functions that may be found in such business-process tools.

Availability of graphic tools

Workflows are often more apparent and more readily understood when they are represented in a graphical format. These tools are used to design Workflow maps that can be generated manually or automatically.

Routing capability

This function controls how tasks or work activities are directed or routed to different work functions. Depending on the sophistication of the software, tasks may be routed on a conditional, sequential, parallel, dynamic or job-role basis.

The establishment of groups

The system's ability to define a group of individuals that will collectively develop a task and define which individuals in the group should process any given stage.

Performance metrics

Performance metrics are the economic values (such as time and costs) placed upon each stage of the work activity. Some systems will automatically accommodate this formulation, prompting the administrators for basic information such as overhead costs, salaries and standard number of working hours and days in any given period. Other systems will require manual programming to accommodate this function.

Queue management

The process of organising tasks or sub-activities by priority in a queue system, as opposed to simply routing via an individual or group.

Management of events

The functions within this category relate on the whole to scheduling issues. These may include an ability to activate a series of processes at a given time, impose waiting conditions, or set email agents to remind individuals of duties required at any given time or when a document becomes available for processing for instance.

Workload

The ability of a system to analyse and display (and possibly set limits on?) the workload undertaken by any given group or individual.

Integration capacity

The ability for the workflow to integrate with existing (and future) legacy systems such as databases and office software suites.

Monitoring

The ability actively to monitor workflow processes and report the progress of individuals and groups according to predetermined milestones and schedules.

Simulation

Simulation functions allow a predetermined workflow process to be run through automatically and allow the managers to check or highlight potential pitfalls in either the design of the work process or in the scheduling values programmed.

Webflow

When integrating mission-critical business applications with an organisation's Intranet and extranet, obviously this function is critical, especially as this interface holds the key to providing a low-cost way of getting a large population to access company information and workflow (Mansell-Lewis, 1998b). However, until business applications dedicated for Intranet use become more pervasive, this is an evaluation factor that must be considered in detail. Assuming the system has a web-interface, does it share the same functionality through an Internet or Intranet browser as it does through any proprietary interface? If there is a compromise in the functions, consideration should be given to how this will affect those workers (e.g. remote workers) who may not readily have access to the proprietary interface (Dangelmaier et al., 1999).

This will be less of a concern in the near future as the predominant form underlying technology for workflow systems will be Internet/Intranet-based as independent programming platforms like Java become more sophisticated and commonly used (Fakas and Karakostas, 1999).

Task management

Task management is the functionality that provides the ability to handle delayed tasks, and the flexibility of redesigning task components or criteria, in mid-throw of the actual work process taking place.

Process management

The ability for a system to differentiate between and accommodate different types of business processes, namely: Production Workflows, Collaboration Workflows, Management Workflows and Ad Hoc Workflows.

Documentation

Documentation refers, on the whole, to the user's manual and help facilities, whether hard copy or in electronic text format. This aspect may also include the facility to print reports and diagrams relating to individual workflows and, where programming is heavily used, the facility to document the code to allow other programmers to interpret the programming when adaptations are required.

Hardware and software considerations

Aspects will include the type of operating system(s) supported, especially if the system is to be rolled out across different businesses that may be using different operating systems. From the Intranet perspective the use of web-based or web-enabled software will reduce the significance of this factor, but even here the software will still need to reside on servers across the organisation where operating systems differ. Any extra purchases should also be identified. Minimum server specifications should be checked, as should any special networking infrastructure requirements.

Organisational aspects for consideration and evaluation may include the following:

Human factors

Factors include the learning curve required for workflow designers and end-users alike to become familiar with system functions. General ease-of-use is also an important factor – can the interface be customised?

Process analysts and designers

Consideration must be given to the level of additional programming that may be required when purchasing such systems. Programmers and developers should be consulted at this point even if no such requirement is yet envisaged. What is the underlying programming language – does the organisation already employ people with the appropriate programming language skills? How easy to use or cumbersome do they regard the available programming functions?

Vendor/product reputation

Determining the current sales success of the vendor will give an indication as to the popularity of the product. Reviews from appropriate trade sources will also give an indication as to how successful the product is, and has been, in providing automated workflow solutions.

Technical support

Playing such a critical role in how a business operates, after-sales or technical support is crucial to ensure systems operate smoothly. A variety of support levels should be available to help resolve any problems quickly, thereby causing the least amount of disruption to day-to-day operations. Aspects include training programmes, telephone and email help-lines, web sites with technical updates and Frequently Asked Questions, and the facility for modem or extranet support where direct intervention by vendor staff may be necessary.

Canvass user needs

Consult all potential users in the organisation to establish whether the proposed product(s) meets the business needs of the respective business function. Part of this survey may include an analysis of the functionality offered by the product (as described in the 'Technological aspects' section). The survey may also wish to include those issues discussed in this section described under the headings 'Human factors' and 'Process designers and analysts'.

Acceptance

Resistance to change will arise in any organisation whether this is a change in culture or the introduction of new business practices or software. Careful consideration and appropriate actions at the product selection and implementation stage will have a crucial effect on how successfully the system is accepted across an organisation.

Trial versions of software are often available for download from vendor web sites either immediately or through direct negotiation with the sales department. This will help to assess the risks associated with the introduction of such technology and provide an opportunity directly to evaluate and compare products with their competitors.

Cost of product

Depending on the size of the company, the scaling of the product across Intranet/ extranet networks and future planned developments, the amount of work in determining the overall costs of purchasing a product will vary between organisations.

Minimum investment packages are often provided by vendors, but the cheapest product from a 'face-value' perspective may not necessarily be the cheaper or most cost-effective choice of the options several months down the line, following the implementation of the system. Training can incur significant costs whether catered for by the vendor, a third party training organisation, or through in-house staff development functions.

The ease in which the computing network can expand to all areas of the organisation through the use of Intranets and extranet technologies does not mean that applications can correspondingly be scaled out across the network. Site and user licences for workflow products (as with many software applications) may restrict access by employees based in other areas of the business. Conditions such as this should be clarified from the start, as this will affect the effectiveness of the solution from the beginning and seriously affect any future developments to extend provision of the system across the whole of the organisation and to future suppliers and partners.

During the evaluation period, seek a quote for a guaranteed price and a list of all the salient licence conditions imposed by the vendor. Ensure the price and agreement will be guaranteed several weeks later to allow an adequate period to evaluate products and create business cases for the purchase of the system. Cost obviously has a significant impact on how purchase decisions are made. Moving goal posts in the form of price and licence agreement conditions will require significant and costly investment in re-evaluating the business case for purchasing a product.

Security is also an issue that transcends both technological and organisational aspects. If the integrity of the data and workflow process cannot be adequately protected then, not only is intellectual property at risk, but also the effective running of the enterprise as a whole may be at risk. Even if security risks have been addressed and safeguards have been acted upon this must be made explicit to all users to ensure that this factor does not unnecessarily add to any organisation-wide resistance to change (Workflow Management Coalition, 1998b).

Finally, in the worst-case scenario, the cost of (and feasibility) of implementing a rollback programme should be evaluated in the event of everything going wrong!

What should you consider when implementing Groupware solutions? Some answers you might wish to seek before starting this process may include:

- Do you have strong integration requirements with existing communication systems?

- How sophisticated are your user-requirements? Furthermore how sophisticated are your users in terms of IT skills – do the two marry up?

- How many servers will you need to implement this particular resolution?

- Insist on the vendors giving you names of existing customers who you can contact in order to check out their claims for the product.

- Is this an appropriate time to consider moving over to unified messaging rather than just seeking the traditional benefits associated with Groupware as mentioned so far?
- Do you require basic intuitive systems meeting a minimum need level or do you seek a system that is highly customisable with plenty of scope for extending developments and programming?

In turn you should consider the implications for dedicated staffing that this may require.

As this is a book discussing Intranet issues, obviously it is advocated that the more facilities available via a web-interface, so much the better! Benefits from this interface are not just provided by the wider access given to remote workers outside the main organisational LAN or WAN, but also for practical reasons from an implementation perspective. Traditional packages that require client software to be installed on each workstation obviously require significant commitment in terms of human resources. These resources are not just required for a one-off installation, but also every time a problem occurs or an upgrade is required. Alternatively, the more sophisticated the web front-end in providing these functions, the greater the reduction in maintenance and customisation costs.

Network Week (Cartwright, 1999) suggest that you should also take into account your current networking environment. Not surprisingly it suggests that those with a NDS-based (Novell Directory Server) house may be advised to look seriously at GroupWise whilst those using MS Mail or Outlook may be better advised to look at Exchange.

The big names in Groupware vendors include:

Lotus Notes (with Domino for web-access)
Microsoft (Exchange)
Netscape (Communicator family)
Novell (GroupWise)

However, if you already have an email system, you may well decide you wish to implement one of the many (and less expensive) stand-alone solutions for Document Management or collaborative communication. The latter have recently grown in significant numbers due largely through their use on the Internet, which easily transfers to the Intranet environment.

An excellent resource providing a comprehensive list of all kinds of groupware, and advice an evaluating such products is available at: http://thinkofit.com/webconf/index.htm

Chapter 17

Extranets

It is generally claimed an extranet can improve communication between an organisation, its customers and suppliers and any geographically dispersed employee.

Extranet technologies and systems allow limited access to your Intranet through networks external to your organisation. Depending on whose definition you read, gateways may be provided via the Internet, dial-up connections or privately leased IP VPNs.

Not surprisingly Lotus take a corporate slant in their description of an extranet:

> 'An extended Intranet linked across multiple partner enterprises, giving closed, controlled access to information between enterprises.'

> (Lotus, 2000)

From an ebusiness perspective though, it can be argued that the more commonly available the method of access, the more readily available the service or information is going to be for the interested third parties. The ubiquitous nature of the Internet then, obviously makes it one of the more popular gateways adopted to enable extranet access. However, the increased ease of access and deployment associated with the use of the Internet also brings with it the increased risk of unauthorised access to your internal network and systems. Therefore, sensitivity of information and the cost of suitable security measures to guard against these threats is obviously a critical issue to be considered when deciding upon the method of entry that is going to be provided to access these extranet services.

In a recent study, IBM Global Services (Poston, 1999) claimed the major benefits of Internet/Intranet deployment to be:

- cost reduction (36 percent of responses)
- commerce revenue (32 percent of responses)
- productivity increase (32 percent of responses)

Depending on the security systems employed, your extranet can provide varying degrees of access rights to internal information systems based on the identification of the respective user or user-group.

Security levels can vary from simple password authentication required of the user, to more sophisticated levels of security requiring 'client-based' software to be installed on the workstation external to the main organisation's network. This further reduces the possibility of access by unauthorised third parties and provides greater control over what information is accessible by the remote user. Systems that use this higher degree of security are often referred to as Virtual Private Networks (VPNs).

So what is the value in providing access to users external to the organisation's network and who are they?

There are three typical user groups who are provided with access to an organisation's Intranet via an extranet:

*   Remote workers
*   Customers i.e. external customers not inter-departmental customers
*   Suppliers

17.1 Remote workers

This group of employees includes home-workers, field workers, franchises and satellite locations (sales offices etc) who are provided with access to the same business critical applications available to their corporate site-based counterparts using remote access technologies.

The Information Security Forum describes remote access as:

> 'The ability, for an organisation's staff, to access corporate information and systems from a remote location, across an external telecommunications service.'

> (Information Security Forum, 1999)

The advantage extended to staff and engineers, for example, is access to a wide range of critical information such as customer data, details of equipment breakdown, organisation product and service specifications and prices, as well as those of competitors, all delivered instantly to laptops, mobile telephones and palmtops.

The number of teleworkers (home workers using ICT) in the UK shouldn't be underestimated. According to the Institute of Employment Studies, 1.2 million of the UK workforce are currently teleworkers and this is expected to double by 2003 (Computer Weekly, 2000).

17.2 Teleworking

The rise in the number of teleworkers in recent years owes a lot to the increasingly sophisticated but intuitive means available to the remote worker in accessing the centralised resources of organisations. Internet technologies have had a significant influence in the ease with which this has become possible. Before looking at those advantages of using Internet technologies to access Intranet and extranet resources it is first useful to have an understanding of the business value of supporting such working styles.

There may be many reasons why an organisation may consider teleworking. European Union funded studies have revealed the following advantages of teleworking apply in general (European Telework Online, 2000).

Cost savings

The main savings are generally acknowledged to be in accommodation costs, office overheads and labour. Any issues relating to office and personnel relocation, at least as far as the teleworker is concerned, can be totally eliminated.

Increased productivity

Both teleworkers and their respective managers have consistently reported productivity increases of between 10-40 percent. Reasons for this are attributed to teleworkers avoiding travel time and the typical and sometimes unnecessary interruptions of an office environment. Less absenteeism is also generally experienced.

Improved motivation

Increased motivation has also been widely reported amongst teleworkers as these groups of employees are claimed to respond well to the signal of trust and confidence indicated by the employer's adoption of more independent work styles that are inherent in teleworking. Presumably this increase in motivation is also a contributing factor to the increased productivity experienced.

Organisation flexibility

Teleworkers are often equipped in terms of technology, skills and experience in the culture of virtual or remote project work. This provides an organisation with the flexibility of rapidly assembling or reassembling dispersed teams to work on a variety of issues regardless of time and geography and with minimum disruption to their personal lives.

Resilience

Disruptions, external and beyond the control of the organisation, such as industrial action, extreme weather conditions, transport problems and natural disasters have little or no effect on the teleworker compared to their office-based counterparts. There is obviously the factor that the teleworker is wholly dependent on telecommunication systems but to a large extent this also affects the central-office based worker equally.

Benefits for individuals

- The opportunity to avoid long and costly journeys to and from work
- Improved work opportunities and the possibility for more responsibility within the work process
- Flexible working hours
- Better balance of work and family life
- Access to work for people with specific difficulties

Disadvantages

Depending on the existing organisation structure, it is likely some disadvantages may arise through teleworking. Such disadvantages (or problems that need to be investigated) may include:

- Managerial or supervisory problems (whether related to delegation or report processes or issues of perceived trustworthiness in the employee)
- Adapting IT and telecommunications technology to meet the needs of the remote worker
- Quality issues and related controls
- Inappropriate job functions being carried out at a distance that ideally need to be based on-site

As can be seen in the examples above, these perceived or actual problems tend to be either of a technical or cultural nature. The technical problems may be more readily recognised through carrying out audits to check whether the services actually required by the remote worker are accommodated by the existing networking infrastructure and the equipment held remotely by the teleworker. Part of this audit should also include the ability of the teleworker to use the technology and identify provision for their future training and support needs.

Security is, again, of paramount concern in protecting an organisation's intellectual property and to prevent malicious attacks on the corporate IT infrastructure. Although the wider implications of security are discussed elsewhere in the book, the following procedural steps and related objectives should be addressed when securing remote access (Information security Forum, 1999):

1.   Agree approach for securing remote access – ensure that securing remote access is approached in a consistent and effective manner

2.   Review current situation - review existing remote access connections in order to understand the extent and purpose of current usage

3.   Develop policy and standards – develop formal pollicies and standards which communicate the overall strategy for securing remote access to all staff involved with providing, supporting or using a remote access service

4.   Understand high-level security implications – gain an overview of current or proposed remote access systems so that high-level security implications can be understood

5.   Perform a risk analysis – identify and assess the risks associated with providing remote access and to ensure that appropriate control requirements are agreed

6.   Establish secure remote environments - ensure that all remote environments from which connections are made to the corporate computing infrastructure are secured

7.   Review telecommunications services – ensure that appropriate telecommunications services are selected, and that they meet security requirements

8.   Protect corporate computing infrastructure – ensure that target networks, systems and information are protected in accordance with their sensitivity and criticality

9.   Implement secured solutions – ensure that secure remote access services are fully tested, well supported and implemented in a secure manner

10.   Maintain a secured remote access service – ensure that all remote access services are properly managed so that they continue to meet business and security requirements

Regarding operational or cultural issues, deciding whether the implementation of teleworking can benefit the organisation in any manner first requires:

•   the identification of those positions that are likely to most benefit from this form of working style

•   the undertaking of a SWOT (Strengths, Weakness, Opportunities and Threats) analysis. If the outcomes appear to support the move to a remote working style then...

- measure the existing outputs and evaluate the current benefits of a specific job function or employee in the conventional place of work
- implement a trial period of teleworking (taking into account the technical user needs audit beforehand)
- check and measure the resultant outputs and benefits against those collated in the conventional place of work. Make a diagnosis based upon these facts as to whether the transition to a teleworking style is an appropriate one for the business needs of the organisation

Ideally the above tests will be carried out initially on a small scale rather than via a 'big-bang' approach. These evaluation processes can then be documented and used as case studies in helping to determine the business case for other possible areas, where the move to teleworking may be considered advantageous for the organisation.

Other issues to consider that are beyond the scope of this book, but exist in detail elsewhere (TCA, 1998; Huws, 1997; Jackson and Wielen, 1998), relate to the detailed analysis of organisational issues and the identification of overall costs which may be incurred through introducing telework programmes. However a summary of the pros and cons associated with teleworking are listed below:

Advantages of using an Intranet/extranet connection in particular include:

- Employees can use corporate/centrally-based resources from anywhere in the world
- Support costs are significantly reduced as only one interface is used i.e. the web browser as opposed to several different dedicated software clients being required
- The use of a single piece of client software also means that in theory at least, there are less technical problems that can occur for the remote user
- The 'point-and- click' nature of the browser interface to legacy systems reduces the need for comprehensive training and allows quicker retrieval of resources

Useful web sites for further information:

International telework Association	http://www.telecommute.org
European Telework Online	http://www.eto.org.uk
The Telework, Telecottage and Telecentre Association	http://www.tca.org.uk/
European Community Telework/Telematics Forum	http://www.telework-forum.org/

17.3 Customer and supplier systems

Typically, any organisation, regardless of its market sector, will find itself in the position of both customer and supplier of some product or service. This section will look at how the relationship between the organisation, its suppliers and customers can be enhanced through providing limited access to internal electronic business applications via Intranet and Extranet services.

Just to give an idea of the interest being raised by the promise of such enhancements, Durlacher Research has provided estimates for the European business-to-business e-commerce market in the near future. Conservative estimates for the value of goods and services traded are expected to grow from:

'...$76 billion in 2000 to $159 billion in 2001, $366 billion in 2002, $766 billion in 2003 and £1.272 trillion in 2004'

(Skinner, 2000)

The next two sub-sections will discuss some of the value-added forms of electronic contact that are driving these market interests in customer and supplier business processes.

Customers

To remain competitive, organisations are continuously expected to improve the quality and range of their customer services to both corporate and individual clients. Extranet technologies also allow these services to be provided 24 hours a day, 356 days a year, thereby providing more opportunity to improve customer satisfaction.

Some of the services that may be provided in this manner include:

- Enabling customers to contact the organisation for information, complaints, feedback, etc., and even to facilitate collaborative working on issues such as joint ventures or Quality Assurance compliance activities
- Technical alerts and services restricted to specific customers
- Enables enhanced warranty options and services to be provided to specific customers
- Self-help/problem solving services
- Automated quote generation for products and services; these facilities can repeatedly offer variable product specifications time and time again with no costly intervention needed by sales staff
- Enabling customers to make payments to the organisation
- Enabling customers to place orders and check their respective status/progress

- Notifying customers of emergencies in the supply chain such as industrial action, fires, transport delays etc.

Any of the services listed above can be implemented as stand-alone measures or in ad hoc configurations, depending on those areas deemed as a priority customer service by the host organisation. The conventional non web-based approach in the past has been to ensure all these options and any other form of contact or customer details are integrated and cross-referenced in one system. This approach is commonly known as Customer Relationship Management or CRM.

Durlacher Research describe CRM as:

> '...the systems and infrastructure required to analyse, capture and share all parts of the customer's relationship with the enterprise. From a strategic perspective, it represents a process to measure and allocate organisational resources to those activities that have the greatest return and impact on profitable customer relationships.'
>
> (Skinner, 2000)

Possibly the recent promise of rewards associated with e-commerce that have been highlighted previously, is one factor in encouraging a shift from proprietary CRM solutions to encompass Intranet and extranet functionality. Whilst some traditional CRM vendors are struggling to web-enable their products, other Web customer-interaction vendors and 'eCRM' vendors have appeared on the scene to offer dedicated web-based solutions.

Any move by your organisation to provide the latter forms of provision may well depend on your existing CRM provision and available budgets, but you may wish to include the following criteria in any future or home-grown solution as suggested by the Giga Information Group (Kinikin, 1999).

Scalability

Scalability factors may include a need for the service to run across different platforms such as Unix and NT. Support for load-balancing across servers may be required in the event of unusual numbers of concurrent connections.

Integration

Any solution should remove as many areas of duplication where possible by integrating the e-service with all legacy CRM systems and customer history. This will help both to avoid the waste of organisational resources and to guard against unnecessarily frustrating customers if they have communicated with the company through web-based services and traditional modes of communication such as the telephone or by written correspondence. Tracking a customer's behaviour on the web site will also allow customer-service agents the opportunity to help customers complete transactions whether these are sale-based or enquiry-based.

Functionality

Functionality is broken down into four sub-criteria by Giga and includes the following:

1. Knowledge Management – this part of the system is an interface that allows the customer to carry out keyword searches of the various databases that make up the CRM system.

2. Email Management – this facility may include such functions as to allow auto-responses in acknowledging the receipt of customer emails, re-routing to specific agents (maybe in another more convenient time zone), auto-suggestions and recommendations according to the contents of the email or the known customer. Other suggestion methods may include responding with a web link to a site with a form that further interrogates the nature of the inquiry, makes suggestions based on the responses or books a telephone call with a customer-service agent.

3. Web collaboration – this category covers all web-based provision including web-form submission and call-back requests. Presumably this will also include Voice over IP (VoIP) conversations if the customer has adequate bandwidth and the necessary equipment.

4. Problem tracking and workflow – this function relates to those issues already identified under the heading of *Integration* and ensures that all history of interactions with customers is available in one common record or in interrelated records.

Multichannel

This ensures that requests can be routed to a 'flexible pool of agents' regardless of the origin of its format. This will require computer telephony integration (CTI). Such provision would allow email requests automatically to be forwarded to agents when not occupied by web-based 'chat' requests or telephone calls.

User interface: customer

Simple easy-to-use interfaces will be critical for the infrequent user of the system or those who do not have the time or inclination to fill out long and complex web forms. Ideally, users should have the option of being able to specify the method in which they are alerted (e.g. email, phone, fax etc.) when there are changes in the status of their request (e.g. a sale or urgent complaint).

User interface: agent

The interface requirements of the agent are the exact opposite of what the customer requires. Hot keys, short cuts and screens with plentiful amounts of data will help the agent get to the required information more promptly.

Vendor viability

As is common with any evaluation criteria of software solutions, the reliability and integrity of the vendor's services should be considered. Giga recommend that the key measurements to be considered are company size, systems integrator alliances, software vendor partnerships, as well as the number and quality of their customers along with customer references.

From a wider perspective, TBC Research suggests that technology driven CRM strategies should be based on the following broad building blocks (Rogers and Howlett, 2000).

- Technology-assisted selling (TAS) – applications that track and manage the sales process automatically from inquiry to completion e.g. provision of sales and ordering activity reports to field workers via web-browsers

- Technology-driven support – applications that automate the service delivery aspect of the customer relationship e.g. email, web contact centres etc.

- Product configuration – a system that allows customers to build customised products where there are choices over product components/specifications

- Database marketing – the initial building platform required for one-to-one marketing

- Marketing automation – a method used for streamlining marketing activities such as grouping customers by geographic and demographic characteristics

- E-marketing – based on analysis of customer behaviour and activities whilst 'clicking-through' web-sites

The UK digital TV services supplier ONdigital, has integrated such an eCRM system with its Intranet enterprise portal to support its helpdesk staff when dealing with customer enquiries (Hunter, 2000a).

When a customer telephones or logs in via the company web site, details are instantly captured such as location, email address or telephone number. This information is then automatically matched with existing data so that the respective customer record is seamlessly displayed to the helpdesk staff providing the status of any current problems or complaints. Depending on the nature of the enquiry, which are claimed on the whole to be 'fairly straightforward' billing enquiries, the system can be set to guide customers into selected parts of the helpdesk environment giving them access to databases relevant to the request and therefore bypassing helpdesk staff.

Suppliers

The electronic exchange of information within the supply chain is nothing new. JIT (Just-in-Time), EDI (Electronic Data Interchange) and Point-of-sale programmes are now accepted as essential if trading partners are to succeed in satisfying the needs of the end-customer.

The use of such supply chain management (SCM) technologies is found across every market sector from manufacturing to supermarkets. Examples may include:

- a press-shop worker manufacturing car panels may withdraw a batch of sheet steel from the stores to feed his machine; this action may then be automatically recorded and inform the steel supplier when stocks are low so that the order can automatically be placed and dispatched
- similarly, the check-out tills of a supermarket may be connected to a central stock control system that records the number of items that are being purchased which in turn transmits an order to the respective supplier to replenish low stocks

However, the requirement of dedicated equipment to be installed, along with their respective proprietary standards and dedicated telecommunication services, have meant that these options have demanded significant amounts of investment. Another drawback to the proprietary nature of the equipment and infrastructure is that there is little flexibility in how these technologies can be adopted for other uses.

In contrast Internet technologies allow communication between many types of computing networks and workstations, familiar and intuitive point-and-click navigation that reduces training costs, and inexpensive software that can be used as a generic interface to other applications.

More specifically, Lancioni et al (2000) have identified the following opportunities for cost reduction and service improvements through the use of Internet technologies:

1. on-line vendor catalogues from which buyers can find, select, and order items directly from suppliers without any human contact

2. the ability to track shipments using a wide variety of modes including truck, rail, and air transport

3. the ability to contact vendors or buyers regarding customer service problems from late deliveries, stock-outs, alterations in scheduled shipment dates, late arrivals and a variety of other service issues

4. the ability to reserve space in public warehouses for anticipated deliveries to market locations

5. the ability to schedule outbound shipments from private and public distribution centres on a 24-hour basis

6. the ability to provide 7-day/24-hour worldwide customer service

7. the ability to receive orders from international customers

8. the ability to check the status orders placed with vendors

9. the ability to place bids on projects issues by government and industry buyers

10. the ability to notify vendors of changes in configurations in products that are produced to order

11. the ability to pay invoices electronically and to check outstanding debit balances

12. the ability to track equipment locations including rail cars, trucks, and material handling equipment

13. the ability directly to communicate with vendors, customers, etc. regarding supply issues on a 7-day/24-hour basis

14. the ability to schedule pickups and deliveries

15. the ability to be more responsive to customer service problems

16. the ability to reduce service costs and responses times

The benefits above are generally concerned with products or services that have passed the design stage of the supply chain and are ready to be delivered or consumed in their respective markets. Contemporary research has shown, in the past, that significant benefits can also be achieved if suppliers or partners are involved in the early stages of the product development process and more recently web-based frameworks have been demonstrated to support such collaborative ventures (Huang and Mak, 2000). Lockheed Martin Tactical Aircraft Systems is one company that has developed an extranet for such a purpose. The secure Web/Extranet site allows managers at Lockheed's headquarters at Fort Worth, Texas, to share project management updates with design teams subcontracted from British Aerospace in the UK and Northrop Grumman Corporation in Southern California, whilst they work on their Joint Strike Fighter prototype for the US Department of Defense. Lockheed claim to have made their biggest savings in travel and training costs...

'We're bringing in expertise when we need it, where we need it, without having to fly someone here to work side by side with us'

(Raskin, 1999)

In researching how companies approach extranet return-on-investment, Stephen Bell of Forrester Research Inc., (Raskin, 1999) found company extranets linked to their suppliers usually pay for themselves in one to four years. This is mainly attributed to efficiencies in inventory replenishments, collaborative R&D and inter-company processing of claims and returns.

Suppliers of Intranet content, in the form of commercial information products such as current awareness and business information, may also provide organisations with productivity gains in updating their respective products. Where once an organisation's Information Service staff would be required manually to load or transfer the latest updates onto the organisations network, suppliers can now readily transfer database and content updates remotely via extranet connections.

Jean-Bernard Quicheron, Webmaster of the European Commission's Intranet 'EUROPA', acknowledged that Reuters is one such commercial information services provider that is permitted 'live' access to the Intranet in order to maintain and update their information products.

Chapter 18

Implementing an Extranet

Most of the disadvantages associated with using Intranet / extranet technologies generally apply, if the means of remote access is Internet-based. Most of these disadvantages are then related to the inherent security risks associated with the Internet, although an additional issue is that Internet-based connections are also prone to frequent occurrences of slow or reduced bandwidth. Security is gradually being tightened through the use of more sophisticated encryption and authentication techniques, firewalls and Internet tunneling (IP VPNs). If your organisation is still not comfortable with these methods, alternative networked services may be more attractive to give a greater level of security to your remote access services (see networked services section below).

A problem that may also apply to Internet-based remote access methods is that some applications may not yet be web-based or web-enabled, or more critically, older legacy systems may not be compatible with Intranet/ extranet protocols. This is less of an obstacle for conventional dial-up connections, as these applications can still be accessed along side the web browser as long as the correct proprietary software is installed on the remote workstation.

It should be noted that the range and extent to which all the organisation's applications may be accessed will ultimately depend, not only upon security policies in place, but on the telecommunication methods in use to gain remote access to the corporate network.

For instance, Intranet / extranet resources may simply require a JavaScript –enabled password authentication process to be completed and therefore be accessible from any web browser on any machine anywhere in the world via the Internet. Alternatively, other resources may require that access be gained through direct dial-up, so that the remote machine becomes connected as part of the corporate computing network. The reasons for this may be either technically based i.e. the system requires your workstation to map to specific drives or because of security policies that require access from a known and trusted workstation. Clarification on such access issues should be taken up with the IS department and / or the department responsible for the provision of the respective resource.

It is also possible that your organisation intends to, or is, providing a mixture of remote access networked services. For example, access to your email account may be possible via any web-browser in the world but access to the corporate finance system to process a purchase order may require access to be made from your home using an ISDN line.

18.1 Remote access 'networked services'

Any method of network access generally falls into one of three groups (Information Security Forum, 1999):

- Public
- Managed
- Internet-based

Public

Public network services are provided by companies who possess Public Telecommunications Operator (PTO) licenses (e.g. British Telecomm, AT&T, Cable & Wireless). Access types include fixed-line ISDN or DSL, standard PSTN via analog modems and more increasingly via mobile device protocols (mobile telephones and palmtops etc).

Managed

Typically these services use dial-up technology to access corporate networks via private telecommunication networks rented from PTOs. These dedicated services include: managed messaging services, X.25 dial, local access services and Virtual Private Networks (VPNs).

Internet-based

Internet-based access is typically the most insecure method of accessing an organisation's network. This is in part due to the relative anonymity provided to the end-user. Although this is a network service in its own right, access is gained via an Internet Service Provider (ISP) using many of the intermediary methods of access described above.

When building an extranet Bradbury (1997) recommends the following should be taken into consideration:

What you should do...

- Find a balance between the sensitivity of the data you want to expose and the security level you need. It is pointless spending tens of thousands of pounds on sophisticated security devices simply to protect basic marketing brochure information
- Think about maximising the function of the applications you offer to your partners using an extranet. Make sure, however, you protect yourself against illicit use of your services

- Replicate data to a dedicated server that manages Intranet and extranet queries. If you are providing data from a core system, rather than having end-users putting it under additional strain, it would be better to have it replicated. Thus, if the system fails, the core information is still safe on a separate server

What you should not do...

- Give people access to content without thinking. Anything you publish to external people is at risk, from both hackers and third parties who may see things they should not
- Underestimate the scale of traffic on your system or customer
- Expect people to come rushing to your site unless your information is well presented and the site well publicised. Is the Web address printed on every brochure and business card?
- Implement a 'fire-and-forget' Intranet/extranet. Content should change to keep end-users coming back

If your organisation has the ability to link one of its internal web servers to the Internet, then it is almost certain already to have the technology to provide basic password authentication systems to restrict access to specific content. Most organisations do not have the time, expertise or the inclination required to build their own VPNs (at least in the short term whilst the technology is still maturing). They do however desire the additional benefits and increased security associated with VPNs, that provide technology functions such as high-level encryption and digital signatures.

A cost-effective alternative to the high start-up costs required for building extranets is to lease the services of the new breed of ISPs (Internet Service Providers) known as extranet service providers (ESPs) (Bushaus, 2000).

Fears

Besides the usual anxieties felt as to whether a project or new initiative will be successful or not, the next major concern relating to extranets is the security issue.

A study conducted across 50 countries by *Information Week* and PricewaterhouseCoopers (Hobby, 1999) claims that organisations who have implemented Web commerce, electronic supply chains and enterprise resource planning (ERP), experience 'three times more incidents of information loss and theft of trade secrets than anyone else'.

However, the FBI suggests that 70 percent of unauthorised access, data theft and damage to network infrastructure actually come from within the organisation.

Chapter 19

Transnational Intranets and Extranets

The ease with which network interconnectivity is becoming more readily accessible and deemed increasingly more reliable, and the opportunities of expanding the corporate Intranet or extranet to geographically dispersed employees and third parties have never been more attractive. With this focus moving from purely national to transnational communication, technology issues alone no longer dominate information management strategies. Greater emphasis is now being placed upon the legal and cultural issues that begin to surface when an organisation decides to connect its computing infrastructure with other networks around the globe.

Probably the biggest overriding factor that has ensured the success of the Internet is its use of open standards and protocols, which are designed to enable information and communication to be transmitted or received across any computer network platform and through commonly available client software. However a slightly greyer area of concern for corporate organisations is the standardisation of 'what and how' content is disseminated transnationally to users based in other countries. Users may be employed directly by the organisation or by sister organisations, or they may be customers or suppliers.

To a large extent, style of content and the technology required by all users of the corporate Intranet can be readily standardised, especially amongst the immediate users such as employees of the respective organisation, even when users are dispersed across the globe. Less straightforward issues are those associated with the national laws and cultures of the country in which the user is located, factors over which the organisation often has little or no control.

Some of the issues that your organisation may wish or need to address when scaling out your Intranet / extranet provision to overseas locations may include:

Language

An example where language barriers may come into play would be an organisation with its head quarters based in the UK but with subsidiaries based in Germany.

So, do you standardise on the use of one native language used by all employees for the whole Intranet or do you provide translated versions for all documentation on servers in both countries? Would this policy merely cover static documentation, such as reports, or would it extend to database records?

Imagine the thousands of documents and communications that may need to be constantly translated and maintained, even if a policy was adopted that was of limited scope in terms of the kinds of information which were to be covered. Even if sophisticated and detailed systems were successfully implemented, human intervention for translations is extremely time-consuming and costly.

Software solutions are available, but on the whole they are still not yet sophisticated enough to be left to their own devices. Those considering adopting such software systems may wish also to consider the following. In the extreme, confusion may lie in a scenario where a statement or transcript within a communication contains a colloquialism such as 'the project adopted a belt and braces approach...'. How would this be translated in an automated process?

Policies and guidelines to encourage the use of native languages in reports and on-line discussions in an international-friendly manner may help alleviate some of these problems as cited in the scenario. Even then however, documents perceived to be grammatically correct by the author may be totally misrepresented or confused by an automated process. If you are in any doubt of the problems that may be associated with translation software, try the facilities commonly available with the bigger search engines on the Internet.

An even more complex area relating to language, regardless of the policies presented to authors, would be the management of conversational transcripts held in active or archived collaborative Groupware or electronic conferencing repositories. Would the policy be applied to these areas of the Intranet or would official interim summaries or conclusions be required, that would allow different nationality users to search these resources?

One company that appears to have been successful in adopting a bilingual approach is Rohde & Schwarz, the German producer of radio communication products (Holzhammer, 2000). With 3,000 employees located at the headquarters in Munich and 1,500 employees located worldwide, the company Intranet sites publish all information in both English and German.

Less obvious barriers to communication but still related to language are variations on the original native form. Examples may include:

- United States Vs United Kingdom
- Spain Vs Mexico

It is not uncommon in both examples for differences to arise in both spelling and meaning of words.

For example, take an international manufacturing organisation that has on-site Open Learning Centres at all their major plants both in the UK and USA. Various scenarios may arise where an individual in one country (i.e. a customer, supplier or employee) wishes to contact the relevant manager of this centre in another country. In this scenario, let us assume that the enquirer is UK-based. A situation may very well arise that a search on the organisation Intranet telephone directory or knowledge-base for the keywords 'Open Learning Centre Manager' reveals that the user has been unsuccessful in their search. There may be at least two reasons for the failure of the system to return a 'result' or 'hit'.

i] because the US spelling may be 'center'

ii] and / or the US occupational title for the UK-counterpart may be *Educational Liaison Officer* or a similar US derivative

From an information management perspective the solution to this scenario would be a relatively simple one. A database with a thesaurus (controlled or uncontrolled) would allow cross-referencing to alternative but related entries. In this particular instance there may even be a policy in place to prevent this confusion by standardising on occupational titles across the organisation.

This is of course only an example to prove a point. The extent to which these inconsistencies exist in practice will depend wholly on the size of an organisation, the scope of an Intranet's transnational connectivity and the extent to which publishing guidelines and policies were put in place at the time the Intranet was first conceived.

These language barriers have so far only covered issues relating to policy and procedures, whether written or as technological solutions. However, cultural implications should also be taken into account when developing and implementing policy. Resistance to change has always been a barrier to some extent in the introduction of new technology and processes – how will a workforce react when it is requested (instructed?) as to which language should be used in published documents and possibly even in electronic conversation-based transcripts?

When countries have two official languages or more, such as bi-lingual countries like Canada, then both practical and cultural implications need to be taken into consideration.

These cultural issues may not just be confined to feelings of national identity but may even arise at regional levels. For instance, in Spain alone, there are four officially recognised languages, namely: Spanish (Castilian), Catalan, Galician, and Basque.

Whichever policy is adopted, with reference to such sensitive issues as language, it is plain to see that diplomacy and tact on behalf of Senior Management Teams will be key to their successful implementation. Educating a workforce, by providing the rationale behind these decisions, can only further help employees better understand why these policies have been implemented.

Legal matters - encryption

It is more than likely that your organisation will wish to stop unauthorised third parties prying into data sent back and forth from one locality to another. So you might encrypt such communications to protect their integrity during transit. Unfortunately encryption is either illegal in some countries, China for instance, or the level of sophistication used in the process is restricted, i.e. the USA.

Legal matters – EU Data Protection

Of further legal relevance to the transfer of information across transnational Intranets, is the instigation of the EU Data Protection directives to establish common European Union rules for protecting the privacy of individual personal data and its movement across the EU.

Personal data is any information that is recognised as identifying any living person from any information held or processed. The directives that are part of the Data Protection Act 1998, include eight data protection principles with which to comply. Of interest here is the eighth principle that states that personal data must not be transferred abroad without adequate protection.

> 'Personal data shall not be transferred to a country or territory outside the EEA (European Economic Area) unless that country or territory ensures an adequate level of protection for the rights and freedoms of data subjects in relation to the processing of data.'

(JISC, 2000)

No formal decisions of how 'adequacy' should be defined have been made yet (European Commission, 2000). The Directive does however establish rules to ensure that data is only transferred outside the EU when its continued protection is guaranteed or when specific exemptions apply.

With this in mind, an organisation must be extremely cautious and ensure that safeguards are put in place to protect against such eventualities in contravening the Act. The EU recommends that in cases where 'sensitive' data are involved, such as 'medical data, and data revealing racial or ethnic origin, religious or philosophical beliefs', an additional safeguard should be sought, in the form of gaining the concerned individual's consent to the processing of the information.

Intranet publishers will not only have to be wary of ensuring that storage of such data remains secure in obvious resources, such as databases. Organisations will also need to ensure that fairly innocuous corporate newsletter items do not contain personal information regarding an employee's personal background, unless their express permission has been sought beforehand or the information is restricted for access only within EU boundaries. Search engines will need to be tried and tested to ensure they do not retrieve such information when used by employees or third parties outside the EU. Employees should also be educated as to the range of information formats to which these Directives apply. These ultimately, may include the contents of emails or attached documents forwarded to countries that do not conform to the standards described by the Directives.

As there is still a fair amount of ambiguity surrounding the enforcement and definitions of how these Directives should be interpreted, the above should only be read from an awareness-raising perspective.

General information and more specific information relating to transborder dataflows can be found on the Government's Data Protection site at: http://www.dataprotection.gov.uk/

Standardising client interfaces

Despite the original concept of Internet technologies being based upon open standards, commercial interests have encouraged proprietary standards steadily to slip back into the arena. The most obvious example of inconsistent standardisation is amongst the two main web browser vendors, Microsoft and Netscape.

It is for this reason that administrators and content providers of transnational Intranets need to ensure that their content can be accessed by all, if not the most popular, web browsers such as MS Internet Explorer and Netscape Navigator. This may even extend to the need to provide two separate sets of pages where needed.

To some readers the simple solution may appear to suggest that a transglobal policy is all that is needed where standardisation of such software is insisted upon and policed throughout the organisation. Unfortunately, the frequent merger of businesses, assembly of other commercial players for joint ventures and constantly fluid relations with new suppliers and customers can never guarantee that each party will be using the same browser or justify the resources needed to implement the policy.

The potential problem of software compatibility is not just confined to browser and email clients. File format conflicts can often arise. Even if dispersed users have the same client software they may still possess different release versions of the product. For instance, an Intranet site may hold Microsoft Word documents created in the latest release of the software but small and remote sales offices or suppliers may have a dated version and be unable to read the contents. Do you then standardise all documentation, to be made only available as HTML pages, move to other easily accessible formats like .pdf (Portable Document Format) or do you adopt a blanket approach and provide a version for each?

A case study: Arthur Andersen

An organisation that has implemented its transnational Intranet using a comprehensive and systematic approach is Arthur Andersen. Arthur Andersen (Swantek, 2000), one of the top global names in management consultancy, went about planning their transglobal Intranet in the folowing manner.

To develop Arthur Andersen's non-US virtual communities three 'Intranet Task Forces' were established and named as:

- Best Practices/Solutions Team
- User Requirements Team
- Taxonomy Team

The membership of these task teams consisted of several representatives from other countries in which the company is based, with special emphasis on those countries where English was not the native language. It was also ensured that each included at least one team member with technical competencies in systems design and ontology.

The primary objectives of the Best Practices/Solutions Team were cited as:

- Benchmarking current process in global companies
- Identifying and evaluating translation products
- Developing a framework for the multilingual approach
- Researching and recommending technology tools
- Implementing a plan for language solutions

The User Requirements Team was charged with the following remits:

- Collecting community feedback on translation requirements
- Discussing content, culture, and community
- Identifying and studying non-English language content sources

The Taxonomy Team on the other hand was tasked with the following:

- To develop a standard for language, including spelling i.e. US English Vs UK English, French (native to France) Vs Swiss French etc.
- Address other language issues - global content, multilingual searching, thinking/writing globally
- Assess taxonomy products
- Build a taxonomy structured to fit the organisation's Service Lines, Industries and Geographies

Chapter 20

Security

A recent survey, conducted on behalf of the Government (DTI, 2000a), highlighted the fact that 60 percent of organisations had suffered a security breach in the last two years. Sixteen percent of these lapses in security were due to viruses and software designed with malicious intent, whilst only two percent accounted for external unauthorised access. However, it is interesting to note that the 'Information Security Breaches 2000' report claims that these two percent of unauthorised access had the most serious impact on business.

Maybe it is less surprising then, that the report suggests that the number of security breaches increase as the size of the company increases. The reason for this increase can be reasonably assumed to be due to the additional number of wide area networks and connectivity between remote users, suppliers and clients that, not unreasonably, provide more opportunities for the occurrence of security breaches. With Intranets and extranets being an integrated part of these computing infrastructures, it is important that any individual involved with these systems is also aware of some of the information security issues that face organisations using these technologies. This section has been included in the book to provide an introduction to some of these issues and possible safeguards that can be implemented to preserve the content of an organisation's Intranet.

When details were sought regarding the estimated cost of any single breach highlighted in the DTI survey, less than half of the organisations concerned were prepared to divulge the cost of rectifying the intrusion. Those details that were volunteered ranged from between £20,000 and £100,000. Despite these estimates, they are suggested only to account for equipment, time and labour and not in the potential custom lost due to lack of customer confidence that arises following the breach.

Of these organisations that suffered a serious security breach, 72 percent declared they had no contingency plans to deal with the event.

An absence of a contingency plan is obviously only going to add to the overall costs incurred due to the breach. Delaying the rectification of the problem is providing increased opportunity to increase costs, due to loss of trust from third parties, legal and contractual obligations, lack of professional credibility in the public eye and loss of public confidence. These factors are in addition to the possibility of the same kind of breach occurring again before preventative measures are implemented.

One way of minimising the risk and lessening the impact of a possible security breach is to have an effective security policy already in place.

Individuals involved with implementing such a policy could do worse than to follow guidelines laid down by BS 7799, the British Standard for Information Security Management.

Overview of BS 7799

The standard is intended to help organisations to implement best practice in information security management. First introduced in 1995, it was refined in 1999 to accommodate the increasing provision of electronic commerce, mobile computing, teleworking and outsourcing. Despite the British Standards Institute claiming that 'Up to 80 percent of the implementation of the security standard is to do with IT...' (Vowler, 2000) these guidelines are designed to be applied to all formats of information regardless of location or physical form and should not be regarded as the sole responsibility of the IT Department.

The standard is published in two parts (BSI, 2000):

- BS 7799-1: 1999 Code of practice for information security management
- BS 7799-2: 1999 Specification for information security management systems

Part 1 is 'the British Standard intended for use as a reference document by those who are responsible for developing, implementing and maintaining information security within their organisation'.

Part 2 specifies requirements for establishing, implementing and documenting Information Security Management systems (ISMS). It specifies security controls to be implemented by an organisation following a risk assessment to identify the most appropriate control objectives and controls applicable to its own needs.

This second part forms the basis for assessment by third party auditors authorised to certificate an organisation under the BS 7799 c:cure Certification Scheme (BSI, 2000).

To gain BS 7799 accreditation, an organisation must undergo a two-stage audit.

The first stage includes a review of the organisation's risk-assessment and the decision processes undertaken in adopting suitable BS 7799 controls. A number of weeks later the second stage occurs. Here the policies and procedures highlighted in the first stage are examined to check their applied effectiveness in accordance with the standard. If the requirements are met, the certificate is awarded which will then be valid for three years.

The overall cost of gaining the Certificate is largely attributed to the fees charged by independent auditors. BSI estimates that certification costs for an organisation with 100 employees might equate to £3,600 - £5,400 whilst an organisation with a 1,000 employees may incur total costs of £15,000 - £22,500.

In making a business case for accreditation, the costs incurred obviously have to be weighed against those that may be saved by preventing security breaches or costs incurred through legal liabilities as a consequence of not adhering to the standard.

Alternatively, there is nothing to stop an organisation adhering to the standard without seeking accreditation and still reaping the rewards of implementing such related systems, as long as they are maintained in accordance with BS 7799. For smaller companies this option may seem quite an attractive one, especially as copies of the standard are available at a cost of less than £100.

The added business value of possessing such a Certificate could however throw a different light on the business case for seeking accreditation. Just as BS 5750 and ISO 9000 are seen, and sometimes actively sought, by prospective blue-chip customers, BS 7799 may be seen by potential customers as a way of safeguarding their own security interests. This may be of particular interest to suppliers or customers who are likely to collaborate via Intranet and extranet connections to and from their own networks.

Data Protection Act and BS 7799

Under the new Data Protection Act (DPA) greater emphasis has been placed upon the organisation's obligations to secure data and prevent unauthorised processing, with particular reference to information concerning 'living identifiable individuals' i.e. employees. Therefore, not only can the organisation suffer public humiliation and subsequent lack of credibility and trade revenue, but it can also face prosecution under the new act. It is not surprising then that cross-references are frequently made between documentation relating to the DPA and BS 7799. The significance of this relationship between the two is illustrated in The Data Protection Registrar's document entitled *Preparing for the New Act*, claiming 'Reference to BS7799 may help data controllers assess the adequacy of their current security regime'.

The Department of Trade and Industry (DTI, 2000b) also cites the following security principles contained within BS 7799 that relate closely to the DPA, in that it:

- encourages the use of risk assessment and putting appropriate security controls before embarking on decisions which would involve losses or damage to your organisation

- encourages periodic reviews of security risks and implemented controls to take account of changes in business requirements and to consider new threats and vulnerabilities

- . provides a number of guiding principles which provide a good starting point for implementing security. Some are essential from a legislative point of view such as data protection and privacy of personal information and safeguarding organisational records. Other controls considered being best practice including management of business continuity, information security, education and training

The DTI also suggests that the adoption of such an Information Security Management System (ISMS) should place an organisation '...in a good position to respond positively to questions which the Data Protection Commissioner/Registrar may ask in the notification procedure' (DTI, 2000b).

Internet/Intranet misuse

As highlighted already, many security breaches involve the spread of computer viruses. Many instances, although not all, associated with Internet misuse are employees downloading documents or executable files from the Internet, which have little or no relation to the business interest of the organisation. Retrieval of such information, from spurious and non-reputable sites, in work time is often the cause of propagating the spread of viruses in organisations throughout the world. Even if a security breach does not occur, significant losses can be suffered by the organisation in terms of clogging up the network, lost productivity and legal liabilities as a result of personal surfing. IDC recently published survey results stating that an average of 30 to 40 percent of Internet access from the workplace is not business related (Draycott, 2000). The American Management Association estimates that time-wasting activities for US companies in particular cost them as much as $200 million a year in lost productivity alone (Whittle, 2000).

So how are organisations dealing with this problem? Prevention of this misuse can be dealt with in two ways:

i] by software intervention that blocks access or monitors usage behaviour

ii] by making users aware of the consequences of such misuse and the penalties both the user and organisation may face as a result

Both methods can of course be adopted by an organisation, but it is the latter that is more effective in terms of prevention than it is as a cure. This prevention can take the form of an Internet Access Policy.

Of course the existence of such a policy is not enough on its own and should be part of an employee's training or induction. An even more effective measure is to insist that employees sign an agreement to abide by such policies.

Websense, a company which claims to be the world's leading Employee Internet Management (EIM) solution provider with more than 8,500 corporate customers, provides sample Internet Access Policies (IAP) (Websense, 2000). Appendix A provides a sample of such a standard IAP.

Internet Access Control

Ever since the advent of leased lines and dedicated high-bandwidth access to the Internet, organisations have used software to help protect their network from misuse or abuse by their employees. The sophistication of today's software however means that access controls and policies have a considerable bearing on an organisation's productivity overall, rather than just being seen as a simple solution to deploying an Internet policing system. This section aims to give an insight into some of the advances in this area of the technology and the added business value that they can provide.

IDC (Christiansen, 2000) believes that Internet Access Control (IAC) technologies are gradually shifting through three stages of technological maturity in terms of what they can offer to an organisation. These are claimed to be:

1. IAC - the blocking of inappropriate web sites and content through the use of 'negative-access' databases where all traffic is checked against a list of known sites. The market demand here was created through legal concerns regarding employee/user access to illegal or offensive sites and content.

2. Internet Access Management (IAM) - systems that block a wider range of distracting web sites and permit the reporting of actual and attempted visits to these sites. Market demand for these systems is concerned not just with the legal implications of Internet misuse but increasing employee productivity by reducing non-business related surfing and saving valuable bandwidth from users downloading file formats such as MP3 music files and video/audio streaming.

3. Employee Internet Management (EIM) - these systems are used across all inter-networked sites, be they Internet, Intranet or extranet based. These systems use virtually the same core components as

the previous two examples but aim to utilise the information generated by user access logs to investigate the user behaviour, not just for policing functions, but also to analyse the use of all information resources. The resources monitored include those held on the Intranet to provide better indications of their usefulness in meeting the business needs of the organisation as a whole.

With a forecast of over 272 million employees worldwide using the Internet by 2003, IDC (Christiansen, 2000) expect the revenue from IAC and IAM sales to climb from $63 million per annum in 1999 to approximately $562 million by 2004 in the corporate market alone.

So what should you be looking for if you are intending to evaluate and purchase an IAC or IAM software package for your organisation?

Typically, a system may be made up of five components that you wish to specify in your ideal IAC/IAM solution.

1. *Collect and control:* here, one of your network servers inspects outgoing and/or incoming TCP/IP packets of data to determine the nature of the request being sent out by the user. This process generally employs both or either one of two approaches: the 'pass-through' approach examines content and determines at that point whether a request should go any further or not; whereas the 'pass-by' approach examines the content that is received from the target server and may be terminated at that point if the information is deemed unsuitable.

2. *Content identification:* this component identifies and reports the type or category of content to a Rules Engine' (see below). Content is identified in two ways:

    i] comparing the source of its origin i.e. it's URL, with a pre-determined control list holding details of known undesirable web sites

    ii] real-time analysis of content

    Both methods have their own particular failings. Control lists need to be constantly updated due to the prolific rate in which new web sites appear every day. Real-time analysis on the other hand may inadvertently block information on the basis that they may contain specific keywords that are being monitored, but upon closer inspection may have a purely innocent connotation once placed in context e.g. 'breast cancer'.

3. *User identification:* this utility identifies individuals or groups of users, checking against the Rules Engine to ensure each individual's rights to access specific web sites or not.

4. *Rules Engines:* this component is a policy management database allowing other components to determine user access rights permitted at specific times of the day depending on the type of content

type requested. For instance, a corporate employee may be able to access sites relating to Sports, Internet shopping and stock trading but only before and after business hours or during lunch breaks. Meanwhile a cohort of undergraduate degree students may be granted access to sites containing sexually explicit, racist or politically incorrect sites for a given period to help support a related study project or assignment.

5.   *Logging and reports:* this final component provides a function that allows the system to record (log) and report all or selected details relating to user behaviour. These may include the identification of an individual user, groups of users, sites accessed, the number of pages requested, the size of the files download, the nature of its content and the time of day the information was retrieved. Whilst the 'report' functions provide pre-defined customised summaries or statistical analysis of user behaviour whilst on-line, there is now a trend not just to use these facilities purely as a policing system but also as an Information Management tool. These systems can also be used to identify the more commonly used (and therefore most useful?) Internet/Intranet sites visited by employees helping to indicate which sources on the Intranet are best meeting the business information needs of the workforce. Alternatively this may also highlight applications and information on the Intranet that is not being utilised as much as was intended.

The Regulation of Investigatory Powers (RIP) Bill

For organisations operating Intranets in the UK, managers who may be thinking of implementing any level of Internet Access Management policing measures should be aware of the recent Regulation of Investigatory Powers (RIP) Bill introduced in the House of Commons on 9th February 2000 and granted Royal Assent on 28 July.

The Regulation of Investigatory Powers Act 2000 (RIPA)...

'...updates the law on the interception of communications to take account of technological change such as the growth of the Internet. It also puts other intrusive investigative techniques on a statutory footing for the very first time; provides new powers to help combat the threat posed by rising criminal use of strong encryption; and ensures that there is independent judicial oversight of the powers in the Act.'

(Home Office, 2000)

The Act will permit businesses to monitor and record communications during their transmission across business computer networks for the following purposes (Turner, 2000):

- To investigate any unauthorised use of its telecommunication or email systems
- To provide evidence of sales orders, invoices or other business communications
- To make sure employees comply with professional practices and procedures often necessary in financial services
- To ensure standards are being met, such as best practice among sales personnel
- To ensure IT systems are working properly
- To check whether or not communications are business related

However to comply with the act, employers must ensure that reasonable effort has been made to inform all potential authors or recipients of emails or other electronic communications such as fax, that these forms of communication may be intercepted. The deadline for having a monitoring policy for the purpose of explaining the use of such systems to employees was 24th October 2000. Policies should include details of:

- The systems that are in place for monitoring and or copying communications
- Whether use of business equipment and telecommunication services by employees is permitted for personal reasons as well as for business purposes
- Clear statements on policies relating to what outgoing and incoming communication is acceptable to the organisation

Obviously, employees charged with responsibility in this area need to ensure that they abide with this revised Act, as failure to do so may lead to charges of committing a criminal offence or risk employers being exposed to possible civil action for damages by employees.

The Government provides a comprehensive range of resources concerning the Regulation of Investigatory Powers Act 2000 on a dedicated web site at: http://www.homeoffice.gov.uk/ripa/ripact.htm

Figure 8. List of Internet security specialists and software vendors

Axent Technologies http://www.axent.com	Integralis http://www.integralis.com	Protek http://www.protek.com
CenturyCom http://www.centurycom.co.uk	Interop Technologies Ltd http://www.interop.co.uk	Sapphire Technologies http://www.sapphire.net
Check Point http://www.checkpoint.com	Morse Group Ltd http://www.morse.com	SurfControl Plc http://www.surfcontrol.com
ESOFT Global Ltd http://www.esoft-global.com	NTA Monitor Ltd http://www.nta-monitor.com	Websense http://www.websense.com

Identifying security needs and measures

The scope of this book restricts an in-depth examination in how to deal with specific security breaches. However, a series of detailed guides and reports regarding the 'management of information security' are available at the following Department of Trade and Industry site: http://www.dti.gov.uk/cii/datasecurity/

Part V

Pervasion

Chapter 21

Future Developments

Predicting the future of technological developments has always been a notoriously risky occupation. Internet technologies could be argued to be one of the most unpredictable areas of all, due to the ease and frequency with which new standards and software vendors continue to appear on the market.

Those areas that market analysts are confident will continue to grow are those closely related to e-commerce strategies. For instance, Datamonitor (1999) predicts that e-business Intranet consultancy services in Europe will grow from its current market value of $728 million to $1.5 billion by 2003 as a direct result of extending the Intranet [extranet] to their suppliers and strategic partners.

The survey conducted as part of the research for this publication also supports this view. When managers of corporate Intranets were questioned regarding their plans to offer extranet services, the responses revealed that 34 percent of respondents were already offering extranet access to customers and suppliers, 33 percent had plans to provide related services within the next 12 months, with the remaining 33 percent with no current plans.

This final section then, will try to identify and provide an overview of the emerging technologies and trends that may influence the extent to which next generation Intranets will reach out beyond the realms of the traditional corporate computing network.

21.1 Mobile and Wireless Computing

Those technological developments that are widely considered most likely to affect the direction of Intra- and extra- networking at the moment are in the area of mobile telecommunications.

Recent forecasts by Forrester Research claim that 41 million people in the UK will be using mobile devices to access the Internet by 2003, with 260 million mobile phone owners across Europe predicted in the same year by Datamonitor (Quicke, 2001). This vision is also supported by Nokia, the mobile telecommunications company, which claims that more people will access the Internet through mobile devices than through 'land-lines'

(Savvas, 2000a). Whether this will become a self-fulfilling prophecy or whether it is just wishful thinking on behalf of commercial parties who would be most likely to benefit from such an eventuality, remains to be seen. Latest enabling technologies such as WAP (Wireless Application Protocol) have certainly failed to live up to expectations according to many quarters of the computing press (Hammersley, 2001; Robinson, 2000; Savvas, 2000b).

It appears that the true measure of this prediction will only be made apparent if the new third generation GPRS (General Packet Radio Services) mobile services live up to the claims of the industry which has invested over £22 billion in the five operator licences made available by the Government. These new services are claimed to offer data speeds of up to 2Mbps (compared to average modem speeds of 56Kbps) and the provision of 'always on' connections to the Internet.

There are numerous guises that current mobile devices take, however they can be generalised as falling into one of three basic categories:

- Smart phones: similar in size to the established mobile phone with an enlarged 'scrollable' illuminated screen (approx. 4cm by 2-5cm) allowing up to 16 characters to be displayed per line. Alpha-numeric characters are input through conventional telephone layout keypads with three or more characters sharing one numeric key / button;

- Palm-sized devices: marginally larger 'touch-sensitive' screens than above designed to except data inputting via a stylus / pen or attached keyboard;

- Handheld devices: examples include the HPC Windows CE as well as EPOC32-based Psion devices with a display as large as a quarter of a VGA screen and keyboard that permits two-handed typing.

    (Zetie, 2000)

Of course, any attempt to classify technology is often quickly left outdated through rapid leaps in technological developments that result in hybrids appearing on the market that attempt to merge the most attractive features of their predecessors into one device. Examples include tablets, slim 'touch sensitive' screens that resemble electronic writing pads or clamshell-styled mobile phones that open up to reveal mini-qwerty keyboards with similar-sized LCD displays.

BG Group plc, formerly British Gas, is just one of many organisations starting to use such devices in order to provide their mobile workers with access to their Intranet. BG employees are currently being equipped with handheld devices that provide remote access to business critical data held on the company's Intranet (a.k.a. KITE - Knowledge and Information to Everyone). Information currently provided on these devices include:

- Telephone directories
- Skills and expertise databases
- Calendar of events
- Latest business headlines and results from services such as ft.com
- Company policies

    (IS Opportunities, 2000)

The technology underpinning these services is the 'Enterprise' software developed by AvantGo. Despite the software's ability to allow access to content for users of Palm Computing, Windows CE devices and Internet-enabled phones, BG appear to have standardised on a single handheld device as their main mobile platform.

Typically, Intranet content is designed with the VGA desktop monitor (and web browser) as the main interface to the system. With such a relatively large display, full-size keyboard and a range of pointing devices available to the user, desktop workstations offer a forgiving interface to poor information layout and navigational design, compared to those offered by mobile devices. Applications on a desktop display that are merely annoying to the office-user, may become totally unreadable on a smaller mobile device. Presumably, this policy adopted by BG can provide dividends in terms of the effort required in managing the usability of content for a single standardised mobile platform as opposed to attempting to accommodate several formats.

Possible technological solutions that may help resolve such problems are examined in the following section.

Web to mobile content

The technical press has been full of predictions in recent times highlighting the rise of mobile computing [see previous section].

With such a great number of mobile users predicted, it should not come as any surprise to learn that products are already on the market to convert your newly published Intranet content into mobile accessible formats. The purpose of the technology is to offer 'write once, publish to all' wireless solutions.

One such product is IBM's 'WebSphere Transcoding Publisher' (IBM, 2000). Marketed as '…a server-side, easy-to-use solution for bridging data across multiple formats, mark-up languages and devices' the product allows current HTML content to be converted to the latest protocols used by wireless devices such as Personal Digital Assistants (PDAs), and mobile phones that are WAP-enabled, HTML-based and iMode compliant. What may be more of more interest to those already struggling with resources to convert existing legacy formats into HTML, is the fact that IBM claim the product will adapt the content of existing web servers dynamically in real-time for instant use by mobile devices.

Argogroup is another company, which, with backing from Lucent and Logica, has developed technology that is claimed will offer content providers:

> '…a technology which allows their mobile content to be read by any device using any platform…'

(Savvas, 2000c)

If effective in practise, software products such as these will bring significant savings in terms of reducing extra-workload on Intranet/web teams and removing bottlenecks, which might otherwise be associated with manual intervention needed if the content was not converted automatically. With several mobile proprietary standards on the market already, such a solution may help avoid future headaches often associated with re-training or recruiting staff with specific Wireless Mark-up Language (WML) programming skills.

21.2 Application Service Providers

As companies become increasingly reliant on new technologies to remain competitive, the risks associated with adopting, often unproven, cutting edge technologies becomes ever more apparent. Purchases of the software licences, acquisition of servers and upgrading of networking infrastructures, and recruitment of staff to maintain these systems, is making the business of keeping up to speed in these areas progressively more costly.

Already mentioned in previous chapters, is the advent of Application Service Providers (ASPs). ASPs are outsourcing agents or consultancies who deal specifically with the remote management of business applications on your behalf and therefore promise to help reduce some of the costs associated with the adoption of new technologies as already mentioned. The benefits promised by ASPs are set to drive the market for this new form of technological outsourcing to significant heights. A recent report by Durlacher Research (Wendland, 1999a) claims the European ASP market will grow from US$340 million in 2001 to US$1.5 billion by 2004.

Before further examining these promised benefits, it is worth explaining how this form of outsourcing is different from those third party services mentioned previously. At the same time, the specific relevance of ASPs to Intranet and Internet technologies should become clearer.

First off, the main difference between an ASP and conventional outsourcing agent is that the ASP runs and manages your application services on its own remote servers and networks (or on the server of an additional third party arranged by the ASP). This is in contrast to a conventional outsourcer who installs and manages the applications on your own site. The employees in your organisation will then access the applications over a network via a secure IP VPN (Virtual Private Network via an Internet or leased line), ISDN, DSL or modem connection. The organisation's standard web browser then provides the employee with the interface to the application.

The benefits gained through implementing new technology through ASPs opposed to their adoption and maintenance in-house, generally come down to the fact that the applications, equipment and support are rented (usually on a monthly basis) rather than purchased outright. This allows an organisation access to the latest technology and respective expertise without incurring the usual labour, training and equipment costs associated with such investments. The costs typically avoided or dramatically reduced include:

- Product research and evaluation
- Implementing the infrastructure and purchasing of application servers
- Modifying legacy systems to integrate successfully with new applications
- Guaranteed security through service level agreements

Are there any disadvantages? As yet, like any new substantial technology-based business solution, the above claims are still relatively unproven. Other concerns also surround the issue of any customisation of the software that may be required by the client. Rita Terdiman, of the market analyst organisation GartnerGroup, comments:

> 'Applications are currently preset with fairly standard templates and ASPs are not going to go through the massive customisation currently seen with ERP applications, although this will change over time.'

> (Lauchlan, 2000)

So what applications and services are available through ASPs? The answer is basically - any application that can be web-based or web-enabled. According to the Durlacher report these may include specialised applications (for finance or human resources), ERP solutions, customer services, sales force automation (SFA), groupware, personal productivity (e.g.

Microsoft Office, Lotus Notes), web hosting, and on-line storage (web warehousing), to name but a few.

It is not surprising then that the services of Application Service Providers are becoming increasingly attractive to all sizes of organisations ranging from Small and Medium-size Enterprises (SMEs) to multi-national conglomerates.

For SMEs the attractiveness of the ASP model lies in the ability of the business to access leading technology and expertise where previously this may have been prevented because of the initial capital outlay required and cost of employing skills to install and maintain the system.

For the larger company it appears that the scalability of the ASP model provides even more appeal.

> 'At the huge enterprise end, firms are likely to go for an ASP solution as it obviates the need for large scale – and costly – software upgrades and standardisation issues across hundreds, if not thousands, of users globally.'

(Skeldon, 2000)

Another application/service that will become increasingly available through ASPs is Unified Messaging (UM), the ability to access all messages through a single interface, regardless of their original format. The advent of UM and the benefits purported to be provided by this technology are examined in more details in the next section.

Fully to understand the purported benefits of UM, an appreciation of the relevant and integral communication components is needed and their value as stand-alone applications in their own right.

21.3 Unified Messaging

According to the technical press, Unified Messaging (UM) promises to deliver the next suite of Intranet applications that will revolutionise the way in which employees manage their personal communication.

Although dedicated and self-contained UM products are still relatively few in number the definition across the industry usually conforms to the following.

> 'Unified messaging involves providing a single interface for people to access the various different kinds of messaging they use. Users can conveniently retrieve their messages from a single access point. Messages can be faxes, voice mail, short messages or email. The user typically receives a notification that a new message has arrived in a unified messaging box.'

(Ecrio, 2000)

In contrast, Lotus provides a more concise definition and arguably a more Utopian view of what Unified Messaging should offer:

> 'An advanced message management solution for all media types, providing access to any message, anytime, anywhere, from any device.'

(Lotus, 2000)

Not surprisingly then, the web browser is one of the key enabling technologies to help UM become as pervasive and easily accessible as its proponents claim. Having a single inbox for all messages, regardless of their original format, allows these messages to be accessed from any technology that supports a web browser making the networking boundaries of the corporate Intranet ever more elastic and even more difficult to identify from the perspective of the end-user. UM therefore, would seem to be paving the way for all remote workers, regardless of location, to be given near-equal access and functionality to all corporate communication as is currently provided to their counterparts sat in front of the Intranet workstation. The remote worker is therefore granted access via the home PC, PDAs, mobile and conventional land-line telephones, CyberCafes, WebTops (Internet-enabled television sets) and public web kiosks.

This emerging market providing technology to enable all telephone calls, faxes, emails, and voice-mails to be managed and accessed through a single interface, is expected to climb from $390 million (in 1999) to $2.2 billion by 2005 (Roberts, 2000).

So what is the business case for an organisation contributing to this market growth and investing in this technology? Lotus (2000) highlights the main areas to benefit from the adoption of UM as being: improved customer satisfaction, a more efficient organisation, reduced costs.

Improved customer satisfaction

UM has huge potential for improving the quality of customer service, whether the customers are internal (i.e. other departments and colleagues), external or business partners of an organisation. More specifically UM provides:

- employees who are able to become more responsive to customer enquiries
- the opportunity to send and receive message formats that are most convenient to the customers
- integration with other applications such as Customer Relationship Management technologies e.g. automated notification of order progress and billing, Interactive Voice Response systems, etc.

A more efficient organisation

The alleviation (or in some cases elimination) of time, location and specific equipment as barriers to receiving and sending messages can have a dramatic impact on the improved efficiency of all forms of communication in an organisation. For instance, employee productivity is improved through better message management, which in turn should aid reduced information overload. With the facility to convert text into voice and voice into text, messages can follow the relevant individual or be accessed quickly from a number of devices, either on or off the premises of an employee's workplace. The teleworker not only benefits substantially due to this factor, but also only requires a single telephone line for email, voicemail and fax.

The ability to receive, store and process a fax using a computer workstation has long been available for more than a decade, but the predicted decline of conventional stand-alone fax machines due to electronic equivalents such as emails has proved to be inaccurate to say the least. Discounting computer-based fax users, it is estimated that there are 110 million stand-alone fax machines worldwide accessible by over 690 million people (Taylor, 2000). In comparison, there are approximately 250 million email users.

It is just as well then, that UM is evolving to facilitate not only hard copy to digital conversion to be accessed through single message inboxes, but also allows the message to be accessed in any number of formats. For example, just as emails may be accessed by mobile phones, converted to voice and 'read' aloud to the end-user, the fax may also be accessed in this way. Alternatively, rather than listen to a lengthy fax transmission, it can simply be diverted to a conventional fax machine to be printed out at a place that is convenient to the intended recipient of the message.

UM may therefore, help satisfy fax users who may not be able to access email or their own UM system and only have access to PSTN-mediated (Public Switched Telephone Network) communication. Or it may provide messages to those people who would simply rather receive their messages in hard copy.

Reduced cost

Reduced costs are apparent in terms of reduced labour overheads. These have already been mentioned above with regards to improved employee productivity. In addition to these savings, reductions in cost can also be identified more explicitly through the following:

- reduced networks and communication infrastructures

- reduced communication costs through: only one call required to access all messages, skimming of all messages permits quick retrieval of important messages rather than downloading all messages
- less peripheral equipment needed when travelling

Additional cost savings may also be gained through reduced maintenance and staff training. This is illustrated by the following comments made by Fischer Unterhemensgruppe which has recently reported on the installation of a UM solution.

> 'Due to centralised and easy to use administration, we have reduced our management overheads to a minimum. Since the user-interface remained unchanged, no additional personnel training was required.'

(Computer Telephony Europe, 2000)

21.4 Instant Messaging

Instant messaging (IM) is real-time text-based communication that takes place between users who have the same client-software installed on their workstations. Short messages are sent to individuals who are also currently logged-on to the network at the same time. The message can be read and responded to by the recipient as soon as the sender has finished typing it. Depending on the software features of the product in use, facilities may include: file attachments, chat facilities (where the words appear as they are being typed), and various user-status information indicating the availability of other users. This information may be displayed in a discrete window containing a customised list of known users with symbols next to each name highlighting whether they are: 'available for chat', away from the desk, and whether they are currently logged-on to the local network (Intranet) and/or to the Internet.

Free providers of such systems are well established on the Internet, one of the most long-standing and commonly known being ICQ (I seek you! – http://www.icq.com). The ICQ client software is automatically activated when the user logs on to the Internet informing the ICQ server that they have logged-on, simultaneously informing other on-line clients that this person is now on-line.

Despite the maturity of the technology, it is still relatively new in terms of being recognised as a business tool for use on the corporate Intranet. Consequently its true value as a communication to an organisation is still unproven. Whilst some quarters view it as merely a time-wasting toy (Network News, 2000), its protagonists on the other hand see it as a catalyst for more effective communication between employees, business partners and customers.

Intranet Digest suggests customer service is improved significantly as IM 'makes it easier for customers to reach you the instant they need help making a purchasing decision.' From the internal communication perspective, the benefits claimed here are that:

> 'Businesses can use IM as a kind of intercom system. Employees can get quick messages to co-workers to arrange a conference call, meeting, or get an immediate answer to a question without delays.'

(Santucci, 2000)

So will IM add business value to an organisation's Intranet or will it merely add to existing high levels of information overload?

One of the stumbling blocks that currently hinder IM's successful implementation as a method of communication between all business clients is the lack of standardisation across existing IM products. Plans are afoot through a group of leading IM technology companies that include AT&T, MSN, Yahoo! Inc., amongst others, to agree upon open interoperability standards which allow all IM users to communicate with each other, regardless of the software they are using. However, the giant Internet service provider America Online (AOL) has yet to be convinced by the arguments for standardisation made by this coalition known as IM Unified (Fusco, 2000).

This standardisation is key not only for those organisations which wish to provide IM-related extranet services to all of their customers and business partners, but also to enable the development and integration of wireless IM services. Co-operation on developing such standards is seen as key to allowing millions of web-enabled mobile phones to be transformed into 'always-on' instant messaging devices!

Issues that open standards are unlikely to resolve and which in some circumstances may aggravate, include annoyance and information overload factors (Schneider, 2000a; 2000b). Messages that randomly pop up on a user's workstation at any given moment could be considered highly distracting, especially as the sender knows you are at your desk and is likely to be waiting for a reply. Others may simply find this an invasion of their privacy. If there is a method of avoiding these problems it is unlikely that it will be merely a technology-based solution on its own but will also include common sense in the form of good messaging etiquette, combined with effective Information Security policies as mentioned in previous chapters.

21.5 Voice over IP

Voice over Internet Protocol (VoIP) is the transmission of telephone messages or conversations over computer networks. Rather than voice signals being carried across conventional 'circuit switched' telephone networks (e.g. PSTN and PBX), VoIP is transmitted across TCP/IP-based networks such as the Internet or an organisation's Intranet.

Initially, VoIP was seen as a cheap method of making inter-organisational and international telephone calls over private networks and the Internet. Even now the ROI experienced by some organisations is viewed as a strong enough incentive for cheaper international calls to be cited as the main business case for adopting the technology (Burkitt, 2000). The UK office of Rainier, the US marketing communications agency, claim they have cut their communication bills by up to 75 percent by channelling their international calls through VoIP. According to Argyll Consultancies, quick returns can also be made on national and local calls. Utilising the existing 512k leased lines between their three UK sites, savings on heavy inter-site telephone traffic allowed the company to recoup the £40,000 invested in the network in less than 12 months.

Despite these impressive returns some business analysts and service providers claim that adoption of VoIP for this reason alone is a short-sighted one (Wendland, 1999b).

The use of a single network to carry voice and data is clearly easier and cheaper to run than having to maintain separate Local Area Network and PSTN cabling infrastructures, but even this is considered to be a mediocre business case by some (Emmerson, 2000).

The true value of investing in VoIP solutions is seen by many as a potential for enabling complementary integrated services such as unified messaging (UM), web-based call centres, video conferencing and fax over IP (Blakey et al., 2000; Emmerson, 2000). Once 'voice' becomes just another form of data on an IP network, as is VoIP, it can then be processed, stored or carried anywhere in an existing or planned communication system. Furthermore it can be accessed at anytime from a vast array of common and not-so-common digital communication devices.

If this sounds like an extravagant claim by the service vendors who stand to gain most from such market developments, it is worth considering the value of the latest 10-year deal between Cable and Wireless and Nortel Networks (Hannington, 2000). The telecommunications giant will migrate all of its network data and voice traffic onto a worldwide VoIP network created by Nortel for the princely sum of £950m.

The IT market analysts PMP Group have recently published the following findings:

'Asked to identify the most important technologies, affecting software development over the next two years, the respondents placed Internet/Intranet at the top of their list (giving it an over-all score of 3.98 on a scale of 1 to 5).' (over the nearest ranked important developments such as EAI, mobile computing, XML, component-based development).

(Sweet, 2000)

A recent survey of 50,000 UK budget-holders suggests that investment in Intranets will continue to climb steadily from a combined spend of £1.4 billion in 1999 to a predicted £4 billion in 2002 (Riley, 2000).

Chapter 22

The everywhere-net

If there is a single overriding theme that presents itself in this final part of the book, it may well be the appearance of these emerging technologies converging to achieve a common goal. Collectively, these technologies can be seen to be attempting to remove as many of the conventional barriers as possible, that are typically presented to users, when trying to access information and communication systems.

The Utopian view is that information should be accessed according to the Martini principle i.e. '…any time, any place, anywhere'.

Ubiquitous Computing

Less flippantly, this vision is often referred to as 'ubiquitous' computing as coined by the late computer scientist Mark Weiser in 1988 whilst working at Xerox's Palo Alto Research Centre (PARC) (Buderi, 2001).

At the time, Weiser and other colleagues at PARC were working on the 'Ubiquitous Computing' project, a programme designed to research the following problems associated with the personal computer. Radical answers were sought to questions such as, why are PCs…

*   too complex and hard to use
*   too demanding of attention
*   too isolating from other people and activities
*   too dominating as they colonise our desktops and lives

Whilst pursuing answers to these questions, the project also involved seeking a solution through the convergence of research areas that had been considered independent of each other up until this point in time. Such areas of study included physical transport, network protocols, file systems, user interfaces, energy management and input design. From this point the project progressed with a view to creating a world with sensors, actuators, displays and computational devices seamlessly woven with everyday objects (including personal attire!), all connected through a single continuous network.

Upon completion of an operational model for their studies, the researchers quickly realised the value of ubiquitous computing (also known as pervasive computing) in the work place.

'Once the network was up and running we clearly saw the vast potential of such a system for augmenting and improving work practices and knowledge sharing, by essentially getting the computers out of the way while amplifying human-to-human communication.'

(Weiser et al., 1999)

More than a decade on from the start of the PARC project, claims of such potential benefits inherent in pervasive computing are still determining the current and future agenda for management and access strategies in the areas of information, communication and knowledge-based systems (Ark and Selker, 1999; Buderi, 2001; Dryer, et al., 1999; Weinberg, 1999).

Personal Area Networks

Indeed, the recent advent of wireless networking technologies is bringing the realisation of ubiquitous computing ever nearer. Bluetooth and Home RF are two such technologies leading the way with market analysts predicting that over a billion Bluetooth devices will ship by 2005 (Evers, 2000; Harrington, 2001). These technologies can be used to implement wireless LANs (Local Area Networks), enabling workers to roam freely around the company premises and grounds without losing network connections on their mobile computing devices. Personal Area Networks, as they are described, may be created for use by individual employees to replace wires that would normally connect the computing device to mice, headsets, keyboards, LANs/WANs, printers and scanners etc.

What are the differences between these technologies and previous wireless technologies such as infrared? The advantages are simply increased range and the fact that the computing device does not have to be in the line-of-sight of the device with which it is trying to connect. This technology, with the combination of the new 3G mobile telephone services, promises the travelling business user always-on access to the Internet and instant notification of incoming messages (Howell-Jones, 2001).

Examples of technologies that are progressing the reality of pervasive networked computing are not merely confined to corporate premises. For as long as Internet and satellite technology have co-existed, access to Intranets have been affordable by any business user via portable devices from the most remote locations around the world. In fact, the only locations where business users have been denied access to their Intranets and global communication systems have been during travel by air.

That is until now. Even this last frontier has recently been conquered and the long pronounced ubiquitous access to Intranets by the communication pundits appears to be upon us. The aircraft manufacturers Boeing have recently launched their new broadband Internet and live television services that can be delivered to aircraft in flight. The service, named Connexion by Boeing[SM] (Boeing, 2000), promises to deliver broadband two-way connectivity directly to airline seats, providing customers with personalised and secure access to the Internet, organisation Intranets, and live television and audio content.

So what does this all mean for the next generation of Intranets?

Pervasion, the fifth stage of Intranet development

The web browser is still being integrated as the default graphical user interface for information, communication and workflow systems at a dramatic rate both within, and external to, the organisational networking infrastructure. It is clear then, that as the different networking topologies such as the Internet, Intranets and extranets continue to converge, and their boundaries become greyer, that the navigation between them and their respective services will appear increasingly seamless to the end-user.

Whilst access to the 'organisation memory' becomes more accessible to end-users, whichever way it manifests itself, either as an Intranet or otherwise, it is more difficult to determine how the remits of the content authors and system managers will be affected. It would seem reasonable to assume that content management tools will become more sophisticated and consequently more effective, but as these issues are resolved and processes refined, what are the new challenges that are being brought about by the pursuance of ubiquitous computing?

Are they any different to those challenges that have been presented to technologists and Information/Knowledge Managers with the introduction of past ICT systems?

The number of access points and intuitive tools made available for information retrieval and knowledge sharing will obviously increase due to the pervasive nature of computing infrastructures and wireless technologies. Hopefully this will continue to improve ease-of-access to information, knowledge and business processes for the end-user. In contrast, it would appear that the remit of the Intranet manager or content provider will require more effort than ever in determining how content and knowledge sharing systems can be provided for the end-user regardless of time, place, and access device.

If we are to believe Kuhn and Becker's (1999) reasonable assertion that the success of the Intranet depends on keeping a check on their four stage-model of Intranet development, the final stage of development or 'integration' is the 'seamless user-access to the corporate memory across the organisation'. Judging by the continued convergence of technology in the last decade, does it not also seem reasonable that eventually this progress will naturally lead to the vision held for ubiquitous computing? If there is a natural fifth step of Intranet progression to be added to Kuhn and Becker's model, then maybe it is related to ubiquitous computing.

Maybe the fifth stage for next generation Intranets (if it isn't already) is *Pervasion* (*see* figure 9.).

Figure 9. A proposed 5th stage of Intranet development

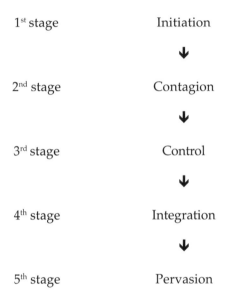

1ˢᵗ stage	Initiation
2ⁿᵈ stage	Contagion
3ʳᵈ stage	Control
4ᵗʰ stage	Integration
5ᵗʰ stage	Pervasion

Entertaining this model just for a moment; if the objective for the fourth stage is 'seamless user-access to the corporate memory across the organisation' what then, could the fifth stage objective be?

The answer to this question may possibly lie in an organisation's need to examine more closely the manner in which it manages the following:

Bandwidth – it does not take a great deal of imagination to realise that the increased number of gateways to the Intranet and larger repositories of bandwidth-hungry multimedia will require increased bandwidth capacity.

Information overload – despite the advent of increasingly sophisticated tools to help manage content repositories and personal communication (e.g. unified messaging) more effectively, these developments will be constantly challenged by the exponential growth of information, knowledge and communications. For the mobile user this problem will become even more acute due to the additional time and effort required with mobile devices to 'sift through the chaff to find the wheat'. More than ever, information on the Intranet will need to be presented in an intuitive and useful format regardless of the device and platform used. The problem of unsolicited communication for mobile users (via the organisation and the Internet) is expected to grow to such an extent that specialised filter software and ASP services for mobile messages have already started to materialise (Hunter, 2000b)!

Security – as computing becomes more pervasive and consequently more opportunities are opened for unauthorised access to the corporate memory, then obviously the challenge will grow for those tasked with securing the integrity of an organisation's intellectual property. Viruses are also predicted to migrate to wireless devices as the technology develops. Gartner Research believes such viruses are unlikely to emerge as a significant issue until 2005. However, this has not stopped mobile communications giant Nokia teaming up with the McAfee corporation to produce antivirus software products for their mobile WAP services (Matthews, 2000).

Helpdesks and technical support – this is another problem area that may become even more acute as Intranet/extranet access is widened. Organisations will need to make sure adequate self-help or support is made available regardless of time and the user's location. Careful consideration should also be given to ensure that third party users, such as customers and suppliers, are recognised and catered for appropriately.

Currency of information – until remote users can be guaranteed constant real-time access to central information and communication repositories, organisations will need to ensure time-sensitive data is frequently maintained on all remote and mobile devices.

In summary then, maybe the challenge (and fifth stage objective) is to manage knowledge and business processes in a way that enables their retrieval, relevance, growth and authorised use, by the end-user, regardless of location and method of access.

Are the future management of Intranets and any successive form of the corporate memory readily achieved then by addressing problems in such a progressive method? As with all unproven models and theories, only time will tell.

Even if this eventuality was realised, perhaps there is an even greater challenge that must first be met by the organisation – a challenge that touches upon each of the issues cited above and practically all those addressed throughout the book. That is, the holistic challenge actually of defining the word 'organisation'. It could be argued that none of these issues can be addressed until the organisation is identified in terms of what and where the organisation is, and more importantly, who belongs to the organisation.

With so many core business functions and services being performed by outsourcing agents, short-term contracted employees and consultants, temporary virtual teams, self-employed employees etc., the term 'organisation' becomes increasingly ambiguous. Under the encroaching shadow of pervasive computing and a widening culture of decentralised decision-making, the organisation and its human resource are effectively becoming an elastic network of skills, expertise and ultimately a membership that is reduced and expanded on an 'as and when needed' basis. This evolution of working relationships, continuously converging and dissipating, has been described as the 'e-lance economy' (Malone and Laubacher, 1998).

Even if this claim by the authors above appears slightly fanciful, many instances and trends of this kind of working arrangement have already been highlighted several times throughout the chapters in this book. Therefore, one of the major challenges that still remains in providing widely available Intranet access, may ultimately be argued to be – identifying exactly who are the users.

The precarious and unreliable outcomes associated with predicting the future were commented upon at the beginning of this chapter. Although the final section is not intended to disregard this view, it is intended to provide a review of the latest related technologies in the hope that some light may be thrown on the more probable developments that are likely to arise in the next few years.

Regardless of the accuracy of the model aired above, one overriding issue that is generally agreed upon is that, in whatever form future Intranets are predicted, the issue of content and the related continuous improvement of processes that nurture the capture, sharing and creation of knowledge, will remain paramount. The reason why technology will also need to be monitored is because technology, by its very nature, will always be transient. Advice on addressing and anticipating such future developments will require organisations to commit resources charged specifically with the constant monitoring of technological advances and the latest prescribed practices for their effective management.

References

Adshead, A. 'Desk portal for BP and Ford'. *Computer Weekly* 2 November (2000), p. 4

Anderson, T. 'Criminal Intelligence'. *Information Week* 78 28 July (1999a), p. 41

Anderson, T. 'Hype or substance'. *Information Week* 75 7 July (1999b), pp. 52-54

Anton, K. 'Effective intranet publishing: getting knowledge to any employee, anywhere'. http://idm.Internet.com/features/critknow-1.shtml. 2000 [Accessed 06.08.00]

Ark, W.S. and Selker, T. 'A look at human interaction with pervasive computers'. *IBM Systems Journal* 38 (4). 1999. http://www.research.ibm.com/journal/sj/ [Accessed: 03.02.01]

Aslib. 'Evaluating the Intranet as part of your Knowledge Management Strategy'. Proceedings from the Aslib conference. London, 26th-27th September, 1996

August, V. 'Intranets are failing business'. *Information Week* 73 23 June (1999), p. 3

Bentley, R. 'Giving a whole different meaning to talking shop'. *Computer Weekly* 19 October (2000), p. 74

Bernard, R. 'The Corporate Intranet' 2nd ed. New York, John Wiley & Sons, 1998

Bevan, S., and Evans, J. 'Managing the library intranet at Cranfield University'. *Managing Information* 3 (9) (1996), pp. 38-40.

Billings, E. 'Simple Return on Investment Calculations'. Paper presented at the 'Intranets 2000' conference, February 28-March 1, 2000, San Jose Convention Center. http://www.intranets2000.com [Accessed: 10.01.2001]

Blackmore, P. 'The development of an Intranet within a college of further and higher education' *In:* Proceedings from the Aslib conference, Evaluating the Intranet as part of your Knowledge Management Strategy, London, 26th-27th September, 1996

Blackmore, P. 'Exploiting the Internet and related technologies as teaching and learning resources'. *Broadcast: Journal of the Scottish Further Education Unit* September (39), (1997a), pp. 12-13

Blackmore, P. 'Intranets: considerations for the Information Services Manager'. *Information Services and Use'* 17(1), (1997b), pp. 23-30

Blackmore, P. 'The Learning Web: a learning environment for remote and campus-based distance learners' *In* Proceedings from the Libraries Without Walls II conference, CERLIM, Mytilene, Greece, 18-20th September, 1997, 1998

Blackmore, P. 'Evaluating Computer Supported Collaborative Learning for the purpose of developing career management and employ-ability skills'.
Paper presented at ECER 2000 (European Conference on Educational Research)
Univ. of Edinburgh, Sept 20th-23rd 2000. [unpublished].
http://careers-main.lancs.ac.uk/ECER-PB.htm [Accessed: 20.01.01]

Blakeman, K. 'The future role of intermediaries' *In:* Proceedings from the UKOLUG conference, State-of-the-Art, Warwick, 17th-19th July, 1996

Blakey, K. et al. 'Unified IP networks'. *BT Technology Journal* 18 (2) April (2000) pp. 44-56

Boeing. 'Connexion by Boeing'. The Boeing Company. 2000 http://www.boeing.com/special/connexion/index.html [Accessed: 07.12.00]

Bradbury, D. 'Extraordinary intranets'. *Corporate Networks* December (1997), pp. 28-32

Bruty, A. 'Tools and techniques to manage your Intranet'. *Intranet Communicator* 2 (1) (2000) [Accessed 22.05.00]

BSI. 'BSI-DISC website for BS 7799'. British Standard Institute.
http://www.c-cure.org [Accessed:14.10.00]

Buderi, R. 'Computing goes everywhere'. *Technology Review* January/February, (2001). http://www.techreview.com/artcilaes/jan01/buderi.html [Accessed: 01.19.01]

Burkitt, M. 'Cutting costs the web phone way'. *Computing* 5 October (2000), pp. 51-55

Bushaus, D. 'Service providers add Extranets to list of specialities'. *Information Week*, (781), 10 April (2000)

'Business & Technology, Businesses drowning in e-mail'. *Business & Technology*, July (2000), p. 12

Campbell, I. 'The Intranet: slashing the cost of business'. Framingham (USA), International Data Corporation, 1996.

Cap Gemini and Cranfield University. 'Intranet benchmarking and business value'. (1999) http://www.bnet.co.uk. [Accessed: 03/03/00]

Carrez, F. 'Agent technology and its applications'. *Alcatel Telecommunications Review* 1st Quarter, (1999), pp. 67-77

Cartwright, D. 'How to roll out a groupware package'. *Network Week* 19 May 1999

Chapman, John. 'Groupware is dead! Long live groupware'. *Knowledge Management* February (1999), p. 30

Christiansen, C.A. 'Employee Internet Management'. Framingham (USA), International Data Corporation, (2000). http://www.websense.com/products/resources/wp/index.cfm [Accessed: 11.10.00]

Complete Intranet Resource, *The*. 'Intranet costs calculator). (2000). http://intrack.com/intranet/costs/index.shtml [Accessed: 01/03/00]

Computer Technology Research Corporation. 'Implementing enterprise portals: integration strategies for intranet, extranet and Internet resources'. Computer Technology Research Corporation, 2000

Computer Telephony Europe. 'Managing voice, fax and e-mail in one'. *Computer Telephony Europe* 7 (4) May (2000), p. 58

Computer Weekly. 'Mobile computing'. *Computer Weekly* 13 July (2000), pp. 32-40

Corporate Intranet Resource, *The*. '10 requirements for a file management system'. (1998). http://intrack.com/intranet/10_requirements.shtml

Curry, A and Stancich, L. 'The Intranet: an intrinsic component of strategic information management?' *International Journal of Information Management* 20 (4) (2000), pp. 249-268

Damsgaard, J., and Scheepers, R., 2000 Managing the crises in implementation: a stage model. *Information Systems Journal* 10 (2000), pp131-149

Dangelmaier, W. et al. 'TelCoW: telework under the co-ordination of a workflow management system'. *Information and Software Technology* 41 (1999), pp. 341-353

Data Protection Commissioner. 'Preparing for the new act' (2000) http://www.dataprotection.gov.uk/ [Accessed: 10.08.00]

Datamonitor. 'European Intranet Services: building the e-business pathway'. London, Datamonitor Ltd. 1999

Detlor, B. 'The corporate portal as information infrastructure: towards a framework for portal design'. *International Journal of Information Management* 20 (2000), pp. 91-101

Dhaliwal, J.S. and Tung, L.L. 'Using group support systems for developing a knowledge-based explanation facility'. *International Journal of Information Management* 20 (2000), pp. 131-149.

Dialog Corporation, *The*. ' Dialog Intranet Toolkit'. (2000) http://www.dialog.com/toolkit [Accessed: 14.01.01]

Draycott, D. 'Security: Net losses'. *Computer Weekly* 6 April (2000), pp. 44,46

Dryer, D.C. et al. 'At what cost pervasive? A social computing view of mobile computing systems'. *IBM Systems Journal* 38 (4), (1999). http://www.research.ibm.com/journal/sj/ [Accessed: 03.02.01]

DTI, 'Information Security Breaches' (2000a). Department of Trade and Industry. http://www.dti.gov.uk [Accessed 14.10.00]

DTI. 'Data security: BS 7799 and the Data Protection Act 1998'. Department of Trade and Industry. (2000b), http://www.dti.gov.uk/cii/ [Accessed: 14.10.00]

Ecrio Inc. 'Ecrio Rich Instant Messaging'. A white paper. (2000) http://www.ecrio.com/products/p_whitepaper.htm [Accessed: 27/11/00]

Emmerson, B. 'IP telephony: delivering the promise'. *Computer Telephony Europe* 7 (9) November (2000), pp. 51-52

European Telework Online. 'Telework (Telecommuting): the Benefits - and some Issues!' (2000) http://www.eto.org.uk/faq/faq03.htm [Accessed: 14.01.01]

Evers, L. 'Which wireless technology will win over the wallets?' *Network News* 29 November (2000), pp. 20, 23

Fakas, G. and Karakostas, B. 'A workflow management system based on intelligent collaborative objects'. *Information and Software Technology* 41 (1999) pp. 907-915

Ferris Research. 'Quantifying the productivity gains of email'. San Francisco, Ferris Research. 2000

Fusco, P. 'Group moves to crack instant messaging barriers'. *Intranet Design Magazine* 27th November (2000) http://idm.Internet.com/articles/200007/na_07_26_001.html [Accessed: 27.11.00].

Greer, E. 'HelpDesk Expert for customer support & service'. *InfoWorld* 23 November (1998).

Guardian, *The.* 'Spreading the messages: soon they will take up the whole office day'. 07 June 2000.

Hall, H. and Jones, A.M. 'Show off the corporate library'. *International Journal of Information Management* 20 (2000), pp. 121-130

Hammersley, B. 'Wheels come off 3G'. *Business & Technology* January (2001), p. 31

Hammond, D. 'Reality bytes [feature: e-learning]'. *People Management* 7 (2), 25 January (2001), pp. 26-31.

Hannington, S. 'A good call for voice over IP: could it be the best-kept telecoms secret yet?' *Network News* 8 November (2000), p. 53.

Harrington, T. 'Slow march towards freedom'. *Network News* 31 January (2001), pp. 22, 25

Hendriks, P.H.J., and Vriens, D.J. 'Knowledge-based systems and knowledge management: friends or foes?' *Information & Management* 35 (1999), pp.113-125

Hobbs, B. 'Corporate publishing strategy'. Intranet Management Report No.10. Intranet Academy Ltd., pp. 10-11. 1998

Hobby, J. 'Special report: security'. *Information Week* 74 30 June (1999), pp. 35-43

Holzhammer, J. 'Transnational Intranets: a European perspective'. Paper presented at the 'Intranets 2000' conference, February 28-March 1, 2000, San Jose Convention Center. (2000) http://www.intranets2000.com [Accessed: 10.01.2001]

Home Office, *The.* 'The Regulation of Investigatory Powers Act'. The Home Office, UK Government. (2000) http://www.homeoffice.gov.uk/ripa/ripact.htm [Accessed: 12.07.00]

Howell-Jones, J. 'Bluetooth reigns again'. *Computing* 11 January (2001), p. 24

Huang, G.Q. and Mak, K.L. 'WeBid: a web-based framework to support early supplier involvement in new product development'. *Robotics and Computer-Integrated Manufacturing* 16 (2-3) April (2000), pp.169-179

Hunter, P. 'Doing the knowledge'. *Computer Weekly* 26 October (2000a) pp. 58-60.

Hunter, P. 'Extranets: opening up'. *Computer Weekly* 28 October (1999), pp. 34-35

Hunter, P. 'Mobile computing: no escape'. Computer Weekly 7 September (2000b), pp. 38, 40

Huws, U. 'Teleworking: guidelines for good practice'. Report No. 329. Brighton, Institute for Employment Studies. 1997

IBM. 'WebSphere Transcoding Publisher'. (2000) http://www-4.ibm.com/software/webservers/transcoding/ [Accessed 30.10.00]

Information Security Forum. 'Securing remote access by staff: implementation guide. October', 1999.

Intranet Academy Ltd. 'Cultural impact of the corporate intranet'. Intranet Management Report. (1999) http://www.corporate-intranet.com [Accessed: 17.02.99]

Intranet Design Magazine. 'IDM Intranet FAQ'. http://idm.Internet.com/ifaq.html (1999) [Accessed: 03.07.00]

Intranet Design Magazine. 'Business Intelligence and the Intranet'. *Intranet Design Magazine* 29 May (2000). http://idm.Internet.com/ [Accessed: 29.05.00]

Irving R., and McWilliams, F. 'Successful Intranets in a week'. Institute of Management Foundation. London: Hodder & Stoughton, 1999

IS Opportunities. 'Powering a mobile revolution with intranet access on the go'. *IS Opportunities* 75 June (2000), pp. 14-15

ISAC. 'Managing information as a strategic asset: corporate intranet development and the role of the company library'. The Conference Board's Information Services Advisory Council. White paper No. 1. April 1998. http://www.conference-board.org/products/intranet-white-paper.cfm [Accessed 04.04.00]

JISC, 'The Data Protection Act 1998. Senior Management Briefing Paper 9'. Joint Information Systems Committee. http://www.jisc.ac.uk/pub99/sm09_data_prot.html [Accessed: 16.08.00]

Jackson, P.J. and Wielen, J. 'New International perspectives on telework: from telecommuting to the virtual organisation'. London, Routledge. 1998

Kenny-Wallace, G. 'The future of distance learning'. *Technology, Innovation and Society* 15 (2) Summer (1999b), pp. 6-8

Kenny-Wallace, G. 'The Virtual University'. *Defence Management Journal* 3 (1) Winter (1999c)

Kenny-Wallace, G. 'The Virtual University'. *Parliamentary Brief* 6 (2), November (1999a)

Kinikin, E. 'Selecting a Web customer service solution'. Cambridge (MA, USA), Giga Information Group. 1999

KPMG Management Consulting. 'Intranets: a guide for business users'. (1997) http://www.kpmg.co.uk/uk/services/manage/computer/index.html
[Accessed: 03.03.00]

Kuhn, O., and Becker, A. 'Corporate memories for knowledge management in industrial practice: prospects and challenges'. *Journal of Universal Computer Science* 3 (8), (1999), pp. 929-954

Lancioni, R.A. et al. 'The role of the Internet in supply chain management'. *Industrial Marketing Management* 29 January (2000), pp. 45-56

Lauchlan, S. 'ASPs: are you ready to play?' *Computing* 3 February (2000), pp. 29-31

Lotus Inc. 'Unified Messaging: anytime, anywhere, on any device'. (2000) http://www.activevoice.com/products/phonesoft/lotus_wp.html
[Accessed: 27.11.00]

MacClachlan, M. 'Push technology loses Midas touch'. *Information Week* 68 19th May (1999), p. 41

Malone, T.W. and Laubacher, R.J. 'The dawn of the e-lance economy', *Harvard Business Review* 76 (5) September/October (1998), pp. 144-152

Mansell-Lewis, E. 'Automatic for the people'. *Corporate Networks* February (1998b).

Mansell-Lewis, E. 'Intranet authoring: chaos theory'. *Corporate Networks* April (1998a) pp. 28-32

Matthews, G. 'The adventures and the perils of the new wireless world'. *Network News* 1 November (2000), pp. 20, 22

Mattinson, R. 'Web warehousing and Knowledge Management'. New York, McGraw-Hill. 1999

McConnell, D. 'What is cooperative learning?' *In* Implementing computer supported cooperative learning. London, Kogan Page. 1994

Midwinter, T. and Sheppard, P.J. 'eCollaboration: the drive for simplicity'. *BT Technology Journal* 18 (2) April (2000), pp. 107-115

Milstead, J. and Feldman, S. 'Metadata: cataloguing by any other name'. *Online* January (1999). .(1999) http://www.onlineinc.com/onlinemag/OL1999/milstead1.html [Accessed: 09.02.99]

Moody, G. 'Look before you leap into the intranet portal maze'. *Computer Weekly* 25 March (1999), p. 53

Mortleman, J. 'Bots clever'. *Business & Technology* December (2000), pp. 34-38

National Computing Centre. 'Survey of IT users 1999'. NCC, 1999.

Network News. 'Instant Messaging thrives in business sector'. *Network News* 1 November (2000), p. 8

Newing, R. 'The virtual HR manager'. *Information Age* 1 (16), 1997, pp. 14-15

Ogg, C. 'Grey intranets in the corporate underground' *In:* The Corporate Intranet Forum. Report No. 3, pp1- 3. London, Enterprise Events Limited. 1997

Ovum Ltd. 'Worldwide market for KM worth a massive $12.3 billion by 2004'. Knowledge Management: Building the collaborative enterprise. London, Ovum. 1999. [Press release]

Perez, M. and Rojas, T. 'Evaluation of Workflow-type software products: a case study'. *Information and Software Technology* 42, (2000), pp. 489-503

Poston, T. 'E-commerce to change view of bottom line'. *Computer Weekly* 13 May (1999), p. 8

PR Newswire. 'Tandy Corporation/RadioShack selects Filenet for Radioshack online'. *PR Newswire* (USA), Apr 17, (2000)

Primich, T. and Varnum, K. 'A corporate library making the transition from traditional to web publishing'. *Computers in Libraries* 19 (10), (1999)

Quicke, S. 'Mobile commerce: a pleasure doing business'. *Business & Technology*, January (2001), pp. 34-37

Rana, E. 'Budgets grow as trainers turn to IT-based methods'. *People Management*, 17 February (2000), p. 14

Rana, E. 'Take initiative on online learning, trainers urged'. *People Management* 7 (2), 25 January (2001), p. 14

Rapoza, J. 'Proof of portals'. *eWeek* 14 May (2000). http://www.zdnet.com/products/ [Accessed: 08.06.00]

Raskin, A. 'The ROIght stuff: Extranet ROI.' *CIO Web Business Magazine* 01 February (1999). http://www.cio.com [Accessed: 24.10.00]

Reuters Group PLC. 'The Reuters guide to good information strategy'. (2000) http://about.reuters.com/rbb/research/gisframe.htm [Accessed: 16.08.00]

Riley, J. 'IT budget survey'. *Computer Weekly* 28 September (2000), pp. 32-34

Roberts, I. 'Turning over a new leaf'. *Computer Telephony Europe* 7(2), (2000), pp. 36-38

Robinson, A. 'Mobile web is not just hype'. *Computer Weekly* 28 September (2000), p. 22

Rogers, K. and Howlett, D. 'What is CRM?' White paper. Reading, FrontRange Solutions UK Ltd. 2000.

Samuels, M. 'Support your local helpdesk'. *Computing* 14 September (2000), pp. 34-36

Santucci, S. 'Instant messaging for the next generation Intranet'. *Intranet Digest*, http://www.intranetdigest.com/Features/000613InstantMessaging.asp. [Accessed: 02.08.00]

Savvas, A. 'Extreme programming in the pipeline'. *Network News* 15 November (2000c), p. 8

Savvas, A. 'Mobile: prime movers'. *Business & Technology* August (2000a), pp. 42-43

Savvas, A. 'Will Wap be overtaken before it takes off?' *Computer Weekly* 9 November (2000b), p. 66

Schneider, L. 'Is there room in your cubicle for Instant Messaging?. (2000a) http://about.com [Accessed: 27.11.00]

Schneider, L. 'Instant Messaging: annoyance or necessity?' (2000b) http://about.com [Accessed: 27.11.00]

Silicon.com. 'Autonomy seals 140,000 seat General Motors contract'. (2000) http://www.silicon.com/ [Accessed 14.06.00].

Skeldon, P. 'Out-sourcery'. *Computer Telephony (Europe)* 7(2) March (2000), p. 25

Skinner, S. 'Business to Business e-commerce: investment perspective'. London, Durlacher Research Ltd. 2000

Stenmark, D. 'A Method for Intranet Search Engine Evaluations, Käkölä, T. (Ed.)', Proceedings of IRIS22, Department of CS/IS, University of Jyväskylä, Finland. Experiences made during evaluation, installation, and testing of several Intranet search engines. 1997-99. Presented at IRIS22, Keuruu, Finland, August 7-10, 1999.

STN. 'Information keep and share programme: how the programme works and how much it costs'. (2000) http://www.cas.org/copyright/works.html [Accessed 14.01.01]

Swantek, K. 'Intranet Information Architecture for International Audiences'. Paper presented at the 'Intranets 2000' conference, February 28-March 1, 2000, San Jose Convention Center. http://www.intranets2000.com [Accessed: 10.01.2001]

Sweet, P. 'Crisis? What Crisis? Conspectus Management Briefings: Enterprise and e-business development & integration tools'. Rickmansworth, Prime marketing Publications Ltd. 2000

Taylor, J. 'Fax in an e-world'. *Computer Telephony (Europe)* 7(3) April (2000), p. 55

TCA. 'The TCA teleworking handbook: new ways to work in the information society, 2nd Ed'. The Telework, Telecottage and Telecentre Association. (1998) http://www.tca.org.uk/ [Accessed: 20.08.00]

TMS Consulting. 'Design and development methodology'. (2000) http://www.tmstoday.com/consulting/intranets/default.htm [Accessed: 18.02.01]

Turner, C. 'RIP Act extends culpability'. *Computer Weekly* 26 October (2000), p. 18

Unipart, 'Unipart enrols 10,000 in on-line university'. (2000) http://www.unipart.com/press/pre_2000_0010.htm [Accessed 18.09.00]

Verity Inc. 'The Verity corporate portal: organize your intranet the way you organize your business'. (1999) A white paper. http://www.verity.com/solutions/cportal.html [Accessed: 04.05.00]

Vowler, J. 'Security: a top level issue'. *Computer Weekly* 6 April (2000), p. 63

Walder, B. 'Unlocking the doors to Web publishing'. *Computer Weekly* 28 October (1999), pp. 64-65

Walker, J. 'Selecting & implementing an enterprise web-based training solution'. Proceedings of the Intranets 2000 conference. February 28-March 1, 2000. San Jose Convention Center. http://www.intranets2000.com

Waltner, C. 'Control the flow'. *Information Week* (739) 21 June (1999), pp. 98-103

Warren, L. 'Your road to outsourcing success'. *Computer Weekly* 3 August (2000). pp. 19-22

Websense Inc. 'Employee Internet Management Resources: Internet Access Policies'. (2000) http://www.websense.com/products/resources/iap/index.cfm [Accessed 14.10.00])

Weinberg, N. 'Networks of the future'. *CNN.com* 5 May (1999). http://www2.cnn.com/TECH/computing/9905/05/netpredict.ent.idg/index.html [Accessed: 07.11.00]

Weiser, M. et al. 'The origins of ubiquitous computing research at PARC in the late 1980s'. *IBM Systems Journal* 38 (4), (1999) http://www.research.ibm.com/journal/sj/ [Accessed: 03.02.01]

Wendland, R. 'Application Service Providers'. London, Durlacher Research Ltd. 1999a

Wendland, R. 'IP telephony and enterprise network convergence'. London, Durlacher Research Ltd. 1999b

Whitlock, N.W. 'Content Management Technology'. A white paper. (2000) http://www.cisco.com/warp/779/smbiz/netsolutions/articles/whitepaper/ [Accessed: 20.11.00]

Whittle, S. 'Stop your employees abusing the Net. Computing'. 7 September (2000) pp. 31-33

Workflow Management Coalition. 'Workflow and Internet: catalysts for radical change'. A white paper. Workflow Management Coalition. (1998a) http://www.wfmc.org [Accessed: 07.11.00]

Workflow Management Coalition. 'Workflow security considerations'. A white paper. Workflow Management Coalition (1998b) http://www.wfmc.org [Accessed: 07.11.00]

Zetie, C. 'Selecting a platform for mobile enterprise applications'. Cambridge (MA, USA), Giga Information Group. 2000

Zimmerman, B. et al. 'The Knowledge Depot: building and evaluating a Knowledge Management System'. *Educational Technology and Society* 3 (3), (2000), pp. 137-149

Appendices

Appendix A: Sample 'Computer Network and Internet Access Policy'

<<company>>
Computer Network and Internet Access Policy

Disclaimer

The Internet is a worldwide network of computers that contains millions of pages of information. Users are cautioned that many of these pages include offensive, sexually explicit, and inappropriate material. In general, it is difficult to avoid at least some contact with this material while using the Internet. Even innocuous search requests may lead to sites with highly offensive content. Additionally, having an e-mail address on the Internet may lead to receipt of unsolicited e-mail containing offensive content. Users accessing the Internet do so at their own risk and the <<company>> is not responsible for material viewed or downloaded by users from the Internet. To minimize these risks, your use of the Internet at <<company>> is governed by the following policy:

Permitted Use of Internet and Company Computer Network

The computer network is the property of <<company>> ("Company") and is to be used for legitimate business purposes. Users are provided access to the computer network to assist them in the performance of their jobs. Additionally, certain employees ("Users") may also be provided with access to the Internet through the computer network. All Users have a responsibility to use Company's computer resources and the Internet in a professional, lawful and ethical manner. Abuse of the computer network or the Internet, may result in disciplinary action, including possible termination, and civil and/or criminal liability.

Computer Network Use Limitations

Prohibited Activities. Without prior written permission from Company, the Company's computer network may not be used to disseminate, view or store commercial or personal advertisements, solicitations, promotions, destructive code (e.g., viruses, trojan horse programmes, etc.) or any other unauthorized materials. Occasional limited appropriate personal use of the computer is permitted if such use does not a) interfere with the user's or any other employee's job performance; b) have an undue effect on the computer or company network's performance; c) or violate any other policies, provisions, guidelines or standards of this agreement or any other of the Company. Further, at all times users are responsible for the professional, ethical and lawful use of the computer system. Personal use of the computer is a privilege that may be revoked at any time.

Illegal Copying. Users may not illegally copy material protected under copyright law or make that material available to others for copying. You are responsible for complying with copyright law and applicable licenses that may apply to software, files, graphics, documents, messages, and other material you wish to download or copy. You may not agree to a license or download any material for which a registration fee is charged without first obtaining the express written permission of the company.

Communication of Trade Secrets. Unless expressly authorized to do so, User is prohibited from sending, transmitting, or otherwise distributing proprietary information, data, trade secrets or other confidential information belonging to Company. Unauthorised dissemination of such material may result in severe disciplinary action as well as substantial civil and criminal penalties under state and federal Economic Espionage laws.

Duty Not to Waste or Damage Computer Resources

Accessing the Internet. To ensure security and avoid the spread of viruses, Users accessing the Internet through a computer attached to Company's network must do so through an approved Internet firewall or other security device. Bypassing Company's computer network security by accessing the Internet directly by modem or other means is strictly prohibited unless the computer you are using is not connected to the Company's network.

Frivolous Use. Computer resources are not unlimited. Network bandwidth and storage capacity have finite limits, and all Users connected to the network have a responsibility to conserve these resources. As such, the User must not deliberately perform acts that waste computer resources or unfairly monopolize resources to the exclusion of others. These acts include, but are not limited to, sending mass mailings or chain letters, spending excessive amounts of time on the Internet, playing games, engaging in on-line chat groups, uploading or downloading large files, accessing streaming audio and/or video files, or otherwise creating unnecessary loads on network traffic associated with non-business-related uses of the Internet.

Virus detection. Files obtained from sources outside the company, including disks brought from home, files downloaded from the Internet, newsgroups, bulletin boards, or other online services; files attached to e-mail, and files provided by customers or vendors, may contain dangerous computer viruses that may damage the company's computer network. Users should never download files from the Internet, accept e-mail attachments from outsiders, or use disks from non-Company sources, without first scanning the material with Company-approved virus checking software. If you suspect that a virus has been introduced into the Company's network, notify Company immediately.

No Expectation of Privacy

Employees are given computers and Internet access to assist them in the performance of their jobs. Employees should have no expectation of privacy in anything they create, store, send or receive using the company's computer equipment. The computer network is the property of the Company and may be used only for Company purposes.

Waiver of privacy rights. User expressly waives any right of privacy in anything they create, store, send or receive using the company's computer equipment or Internet access. User consents to allow company personnel access to and review of all materials created, stored, sent or received by User through any Company network or Internet connection.

Monitoring of computer and Internet usage. The Company has the right to monitor and log any and all aspects of its Computer system including, but not limited to, monitoring Internet sites visited by Users, monitoring chat and newsgroups, monitoring file downloads, and all communications sent and received by users.

Blocking sites with inappropriate content.

The Company has the right to utilize software that makes it possible to identify and block access to Internet sites containing sexually explicit or other material deemed inappropriate in the workplace.

Acknowledgement of Understanding

I have read and agree to comply with the terms of this policy governing the use of <<company>>'s computer network. I understand that violation of this policy may result in disciplinary action, including possible termination and civil and criminal penalties.

Signature: .... Date: ....

Printed name: ....

Further reading

Groupwork, Content Management and Workflow

Anderson, M. and Allen R. 'Workflow interoperability: enabling e-commerce'. Workflow Management Coalition. 1999 http://www.wfmc.org [Accessed: 07.11.00]

Bouras, C. et al. 'A co-operative environment for local government: an Internet-Intranet approach'. *Telematics and Informatics* 16 (1999) pp. 75-89

Bradbury, D. 'Win business with web content'. *Computer Weekly* 7 December (2000), pp. 92, 94

Fayyad, U. 'The Technology Review ten: data mining'. *Technology Review*, January/February, (2001). http://www.techreview.com/artcilaes/jan01/TR10_fayyad.html [Accessed: 01.19.01]

Guyatt, H. 'Content management software is in demand'. *Computing* 4 January (2001), p. 31

Hendrinkse, J. 'Managing a corporate Internet/Intranet: web object management or document management?' *IS Opportunities* 55, October (1998), pp. 14-17

Hutton, J. 'Workflow solutions'. *BT Technol J* 17 (4) October (1999), pp. 58-64

Ramanathan, J. 'Document management systems and how they relate to emergent work management technology'. (1998) http://www.docmanage.com/Issue/NovemberDecember98/dmsystms.htm [Accessed:29.06.00]

Sgouropoulou, C. et al. 'Acquiring working knowledge through asynchronous multimedia conferencing'. *Educational Technology & Society* 3(3) (2000). http://ifets.ieee.org/periodical/vol_3_2000/a06.html [Accessed: 17.08.00]

Workflow Management Coalition. 'Workflow and Internet: catalysts for radical change'. A white paper. Workflow Management Coalition (1998) http://www.wfmc.org [Accessed: 07.11.00]

Workflow Management Coalition. 'Workflow security considerations'. A white paper. Workflow Management Coalition (1998) http://www.wfmc.org [Accessed: 07.11.00]

Departmental Applications

Irish, C. 'Web-enabled call centre'. *BT Technology Journal* 18 (2) April (2000), pp. 65-71

Latham, S. 'Intranets: a UK government libraries perspective'. Proceedings of the 66th IFLA Council and General Conference, Jerusalem, -18th August, (2000).
http://ifla.org/IV/ifla66/papers/002-131e.htm [Accessed: 24.10.00]

Zhang, Y. and Chen, H. 'A knowledge-based dynamic job-scheduling in low-volume/high-variety manufacturing'. *Artificial Intelligence in Engineering* 13, pp. 241-249

Extranets

Barnett, S. 'Top 10 challenges to securing a network'. *Network Security* 1 January 2000, pp. 14-16

Biddlecombe, L. 'The VPN dilemma'. Business & Technology December (2000), pp. 52-56

Cisco Systems Inc. 'Intranet/Extranet VPNs: making a case for secure, cost-effective managed network services'. (2000) http://wwwij.cisco.com [Accessed 29.06.00]

Cooper, M. 'ISPs: find your perfect ISP partner' (special report). *Network Week* 9 June (1999), pp. 37-39

Higgins, K.J. 'Use some ESP: new vision for Extranet services emerges'. *Internet Week* 802 Feb 28 (2000)

Kaufman, E. and Newman, A. 'Implementing IPsec: making security work on VPNs, Intranets and Extranets'. New York, John Wiley & Sons.1999

Lewis, J. 'Extranet security should be a standard investment'. *Internet Week* 770 June 21, (2000)

Pakstas, A. 'Towards electronic commerce via science park multi-Extranets'. *Computer Communications* 22 (14), 15 September (1999), pp. 1351-1363

Park, K.H. and Favrel, J. 'Virtual Enterprise - Information System and Networking Solution'. *Computers & Industrial Engineering* 37 (1-2), October (1999), pp. 441-444

Raskin, A. 'The ROIght stuff: Extranet ROI'. (1999)

CIO Web Business Magazine Feb.1, 1999. http://www.cio.com [Accessed: 24.10.00]

Salamone, S. 'VPNs enter: the Extranet realm'. *Internet Week* 812 May 08, (2000)

Wright, M.A. 'Virtual Private Network Security'. *Network Security* 7 1 July (2000), pp. 11-14

Information Overload

Davenport, T. 'Overload redux'. *CIO Magazine* 01 October (1999). http://www.cio.com/archive/100199_think_content.html [Accessed: 07.11.00]

Kerka, S. 'Myths and realities: information management'. U.S. Department of Education. (1997) http://www.ericacve.org/docs/mr00009.htm [Accessed: 09.01.01]

Intranet Design

Rutherford, E. 'Is this anyway to build an Intranet?' *CIO Magazine* April 1 (2000). http://www2.cio.com/archive/040100_intranet_content.html [Accessed: 20.11.00]

Schneider, A. and Davis, C. 'Intranet architecture: integrating information design with business planning'. (2000) http://intrack.com/intranet/iarchi.shtml [Accessed 22.05.00]

Intranet Management

Cisco Systems Inc. 'Cisco employee connection: exploring the frontiers of Intranet technology'. Cisco Systems Inc., 1999. http://wwwij.cisco.com/warp/public/cc/corp/mkt/gnb/gen/intra_wp.htm [Accessed: 06/29/00]

Hapgood, F. 'The next generation'. *CIO Web Business Magazine* 1 March (1999). http://www.cio.com [Accessed: 20.11.00]

Hong, J. W. K. et al ' WebTrafMon: Web-based Internet/Intranet network traffic monitoring and analysis system'. *Computer Communications* 22 (14), 15 September (1999), pp. 1333-1342

Waltner, C. 'Intranet ROI'. *Information Week* 735 May 24 (1999)

Miscellaneous

Collingridge, R.and Harris, N.D. 'Intranet Advantage'. *BT Technology Journal* 18 (2), April (2000), pp. 87-92

Hoffman, R. 'Web application servers' (special report). *Network Week* 9 June (1999), pp. 31-34

Mobile Technologies and Teleworking

Kaasinen, E. et al 'Two approaches to bringing Internet services to WAP devices'. *Computer Networks* 33 (1-6), June (2000), pp. 231-246

Retrieval Technologies

Bradbury, D. 'Push technology: don't call us, we'll call you'. *Corporate Networks* June (1998), pp. 34-37

Moody, G. 'Hunting down tomorrow's agents'. *Computer Weekly* 20 January (2000), p. 46

Security (and data protection)

Classe, A. 'Rallying to the standard'. *Computer Weekly* 6 April (2000), pp. 48-50

Harris, B. and Hunt, R. 'TCP/IP security threats and attack methods'. *Computer Communications* 22 (10), 25 June (1999), pp. 885-897

Ludlow, D. 'SSL can boost online security without slowing the network down'. *Network News* 15 November (2000), p. 45

Mason, P. 'Beware the insiders'. *Computer Weekly* 13 April (2000), pp. 32,34

Training and Education

Faraj, I. et al. 'An industry foundation classes Web-based collaborative construction computer environment: WISPER'. *Automation in Construction* 10 (1), November (2000), pp. 79-99

Wilkins, B. and Barrett, J. 'The virtual construction site: a web-based teaching/learning environment in construction technology'. *Automation in Construction* 10 (1), November (2000), pp. 169-179

Transnational Intranets

Mullich, J. 'Prescription for heading off culture clash: pharmaceutical giant Novartis taps intranet to ease merger'. *PC Week Online* 23.12.97 http://www.zdnet.com [Accessed 24.10.00]

Index

acceptance of workflow products 96

access, barriers to 25-8

    access points 25

    cultural aspects 25-6

    Xerox case study 26-8

ActiveIntranet Plc. 57

Adshead, A. 33

Alcatel 31

America Online 141

American Management Association 125

analysts, and workflow 95

Anderson, T. 34, 35

Anton, K. 72

Application Service Providers (ASPs) 135-7

Argogroup 135

Argyll Consultancies 142

Ark, W.S. 145

Arthur Andersen case study 120-1

Aslib 4

AT&T 113, 141

August, V. 36

authoring software 57-8

Autonomy 33, 34

AvantGo 134

Axent Technologies 129

bandwidth, increasing 147

Becker, A. 5, 84, 146, 147

Bell Atlantic Corporation 50, 89-90

Bentley, R. 27

Bernard, R. 7

Bevan, S. 45

BG Group Plc 133

Billings, E. 13

Blackmore, P. 33, 37, 45, 50, 89

Blakeman, K. 45

Blakey, K. 142

Bluetooth 145

Boeing Corporation 146

BP-Amoco 33

Bradbury, D. 113

British Aerospace 47, 48, 110

British Telecom 90-1, 113

browsing, selective 82

Bruty, A. 61

BS 7799 standard 123-4

Buderi, R. 144, 145

Burkitt, M. 142

Bushaus, D. 114

Business & Technology 78

business applications 44-51

    information services 45-6

    IT department 46-7

    library services 45-6

    personnel department 44-5

    training 47-51

business intelligence information 39-40

Cable & Wireless 113, 142

Cadbury's 49

Campbell, I. 17

Cap Gemeni 19, 21, 24, 36, 56

Carrez, F. 31

Cartwright, D. 98

CC list, use of 78, 80-1

CenturyCom 129

Check Point 129

check-in/check-out facility in electronic DMS 65

Chemical Abstracts 38-9

Christiansen, C.A. 126-7

Christopherson, K. 70

Cisco Systems 50, 68

client/server costs 11-12

Codling, P. 21

commercial information 38-9

Communicator (Netscape) 98

Complete Intranet Resource 64

Computer Aid 35

Computer Technology Research Corporation 32

Computer Telephony Europe 140

computer telephony integration (CTI) 107

Computer Weekly 100

computer-supported collaborative working (CSCW) 85-6, 88-91

conferencing software 91

Connexion (Boeing) 146

contagion stage 9, 23-51

    access, barriers to 25-8

    business applications 44-51

    content 36-43

critical mass, achieving 24

information supply and retrieval 29-35

content

authorisers 62

creation costs 12

of intranet 36-43

business intelligence information 39-40

commercial information 38-9

flat 36-7

interactive 37-8, 73

see also content management; legacy systems

media options 74

for multiple audiences 73

providers 62

in 'sound bites' 72

content management 55-71

electronic document management systems 63-9

check-in/check-out facility 65

file expiration dates 67-9

file interdependencies 66

metadata, storage 64-5

multiple file type support 67

open standard interfaces 66-7

search and indexing 66

security 65

structure and organisational capability 67

version control 64

enhancing content 72-4

and extranets 69-71

groupware for 92

ownership 55-8

security 127-8

structures 59-63

content authorisers 62

content providers 62

editorial board 62

information owners 60-1

Intranet Management Group (IMG) 62

intranet technical sub-committee 63

local developers 60

local managers 59-60

service provider 63

webmaster and team 59

control stage 9, 53-82

content management 55-71

enhancing content 72-4

information overload 76-82

procedures 54

publishing policy, implementation 75

Coote, T. 56

Corporate Intranet Resource 11

costs

of Document Management Systems 68-9

of intranet 11-17

savings, extranets 101

unified messaging 139-40

of web browsers 7-8

of workflow products 96-8

Cranfield University 24, 36

critical mass, achieving 24

Curry, A. 28

customer extranet systems 105-9

functionality 107

integration 106-7

multichannel 107

scalability 106

user interfaces 107-8

vendor viability 108-9

Customer Relationship Management (CRM) 106, 108

Damsgaard, J. 9

Dangelmaier, W. 92, 94

Data Protection Act 118, 124-5

Datamonitor 21, 132

Deibert, J. 56

designers, and workflow 95

Detlor, B. 32

Dhaliwal, J.S. 85

Dialog Corporation 39

Direckens, I. 81

Document Management Systems 67-9

documentation

conversion of to HTML 42-3

of workflow products 95

Domino (Lotus Notes) 98

Dow Chemical 50, 51

Draycott, D. 125

Dryer, D.C. 145

Durlacher Research 105-6, 135, 136

Ecrio Inc. 137-8

editorial board for content management 62

education *see* training

e-learning 47-51

electronic document management systems 63-9

check-in/check-out facility 65

file expiration dates 67-9

file interdependencies 66

metadata, storage 64-5

multiple file type support 67

open standard interfaces 66-7

search and indexing 66

security 65

structure and organisational capability 67

version control 64

email

filters for 79

notification systems 68

productivity gains using 76-7

Emmerson, B. 142

Employee Internet Management (EIM) 126

encryption in transnational extranets 118

Enterprise Information Portal (EIP) 32-3

Essex Police 34

EU data protection 118-19

Eureka (Xerox intranet) 26-8

European Commission 111, 116

European Community Telework/Telematics Forum 104

European Telework Online 101, 104

Evans, J. 45

event management in WfMS 93

Evers, L. 145

Exchange (Microsoft) 98

extranets 6, 99-111

and content management 69-71

customer systems 105-9

functionality 107

integration 106-7

multichannel 107

scalability 106

user interfaces 107-8

vendor viability 108-9

implementation 112-14

remote workers 100

supplier systems 109-11

teleworking 101-4

transnational 115-21

WfMS on 92

Fakas, G. 94

Federal Bureau of Investigation (FBI) 114

Feldman, S. 64

Ferris Research 76-7, 81

File Transfer Protocol (FTP) 6

FileNET 69

files

expiration dates 67-9

interdependencies 66

multiple types, in content management 67

Fischer Unterhemensgruppe 140

flat content 36-7

Ford Motor Co. 33, 75

Forrester Research 68, 132

functionality of customer extranets 107

Fusco, P. 141

GartnerGroup 136

General Motors 34

General Packet Radio Services 133

Giga Information Group 35, 107

Global Ltd. 129

Gopher 6

graphic tools for WfMS 93

Greer, E. 46

group support systems 85

groups, establishment of 93

groupware 87-98

    computer-supported collaborative working 88-91

    defined 87-8

    shared reference library 88

    workflow management systems 91-8

Groupwise (Novell) 98

Guardian 77

Hall, H. 45

Hammersley, B. 133

Hammond, D. 50

handheld devices 133

Hannington, S. 142

hardware, and workflow products 95

Harrington, T. 145

helpdesks 148

    outsourcing 46-7

Hendriks, P.H.J. 33, 84

Hobbs, B. 10

Hobby, J. 114

Holzhammer, J. 116

Home Office 128

Home RF 145

hot-links 73

Howell-Jones, J. 145

Howlett, D. 108

Huang, G.Q. 110

human factors in workflow products 95

Hunter, P. 35, 70-1, 108, 148

Huws, U. 104

Hypertext Mark-up Language (HTML) 42

    in content management 57-8

Hypertext Transfer Protocol 6, 7

IBM 19, 99, 134-5

implementation models 9-10

indexing in electronic DMS 66

Info Technology Supply Ltd 41

information, currency of 148

information applications 45-6

Information Fatigue Syndrome 77

information overload 76-82, 147-8

    email filters in 79

    personal policy 80-1

    selective browsing 82

    'spam', rerouting 79-80

    training 81-2

    unsubscribe to services 80

information owners 60-1

Information Security Forum 100, 103, 113

Information Security Management Systems (ISMS) 123, 125

Information Server (Verity) 34

information supply and retrieval 29-35

    intelligent agents 31

    portals 32-4

    purchasing 34-5

    search engines 29-31

Information Week 114

initiation stage 9, 10

instant messaging 140-1

Institute of Personnel and Development (IPD) 51

Integralis 129

integration

    capacity of WfMS 93

    of customer extranets 106-7

integration stage 9, 83-130

    extranets 99-111

    implementation 112-14

    groupware 87-98

    knowledge management 84-6

    security 122-30

    transnational intranets/extranets 115-21

intelligent agents 31

interactive content 37-8, 73

International Data Corporation (IDC) 126-7

International Telework Association 104

internet access control (IAC) 126-8

Internet Access Management (IAM) 126, 127-8

Internet Access Policies (IAP) 126, 161-4

Internet Explorer (Microsoft) 119

internet misuse 125-6

Internet Relay Chat (IRC) 7

internet-based networked services 113-14

Interop Technologies Ltd. 129

Interwoven 69

intranet

    benefits of 8

    defined 4-6

misuse of 125-6

technical sub-committee 63

technology of 6-7

Intranet Academy 28

Intranet Design Magazine 5, 39

Intranet Digest 141

Intranet Management Group (IMG) 62

Intranet Toolkit 39

Irving, R. 6

ISAC 45

IT departments, applications 46-7

Jackson, P.J. 104

JISC 116

Jones, A.M. 45

junk mail 78

Karakostas, B. 94

Kenny-Wallace, G. 47-9

Kinikin, E. 106

Knowledge and Information to Everyone (KITE) 133-4

Knowledge First (Computer Aid) 35

knowledge management

definition 85-6

integrating 84-6

intelligent agents for 31

search engines for 30-1

Knowledge Server (Autonomy) 34

KPMG 8

Kuhn, O. 5, 84, 146, 147

Lancaster University

Careers Department

IT support 46-7

ROI case study 14-16

internet, learning 48

Lancioni, R.A. 109

language problems in transnational extranets 115-18

Laubacher, R.J. 149

Lauchlan, S. 136

legacy systems 40-3

converting existing documentation 42-3

launching 41-2

LEXIS-NEXUS 39

Library and Information Services (LIS) 45-6

Livelink (Open Text) 68

local developers of content 60

local managers of content 59-60

Lockheed Martin Tactical Aircraft Systems 110

London Underground 61

Lotus Inc. 99, 138

Lotus Notes 33, 34, 50, 98, 137

MacClachlan, M. 34

Mak, K.L. 110

Malone, T.W. 149

managed networked services 113

Mansell-Lewis, E. 8, 56, 94

Mattinson, R. 84

McConnell, D. 90

McWilliams, F. 6

metadata, storage in electronic DMS 64-5

Microsoft 98, 119

Midwinter, T. 90

Milstead, J. 64

mobile computing 132-5

monitoring of workflow 94

Moody, G. 34

Morse Group Ltd. 129

Mortleman, J. 31

motivation for teleworking 101

MSN 141

multichannel customer extranet systems 107

Ncompass 68

Nestlé Foods 50-1

Netscape 98

Netscape Navigator 57, 119

Network News 140

Network Week 98

networking infrastructure costs 12

Newing, R. 45

Nokia 132

Nortel Networks 142

Northrop Grumman Corporation 110

NovaSoft 56

Novell 98

NTA Monitor Ltd. 129

Ogg, C. 10

ONDigital 108

open database connectivity (ODBC) 33, 34

open standard interfaces in electronic DMS 66-7

Open Text 68

Open University 48

organisational flexibility in teleworking 101

outsourcing 18-21

   helpdesk 46-7

   issues 19

Ovum, Ltd. 85

palm-sized devices 133

Panagon Web Services (FileNET) 69

Participant Server Eprise 68-9

Perez, M. 92

performance metrics of WfMS 93

personal area networks 145-6

Personal Digital Assistants (PDAs) 134, 138

personnel applications 44-5

pervasion 131-49

    Application Service Providers 135-7

    fifth stage of intranet development 146-9

    instant messaging 140-1

    mobile and wireless computing 132-5

    unified messaging 137-40

    voice over IP 142-3

Plumtree 33

PMP Group 142-3

Portal Product Suite (Verity) 33

'Portal-in-a-Box' (Autonomy) 33

portals 32-4

    purchasing 34-5

Poston, T. 99

PowerPoint 42

PR Newswire 69

PricewaterhouseCoopers 21, 114

Primich, T. 45, 75

process management in WfMS 94

productivity in teleworking 101

Protek 129

public networked services 113

publishing policy, implementation 75

'push' and 'pull' models of information provision 29

queue management in WfMS 93

Quicheron, J.-B. 111

Quicke, S. 132

Rana, E. 51

Rapoza, J. 34

Raskin, A. 111

Regulation of Investigatory Powers Act (2000) 128-9

remote-access 'networked services' 113-14

resilience in teleworking 102

return-on-investment (ROI) 13-17

    calculating 13-14

    case study 14-16

Reuters 77

Roberts, I. 138

Robinson, A. 133

Rogers, K. 108

Rohde & Schwarz 116

Rojas, T. 92

routing capability in WfMS 93

Samuels, M. 46, 47

Santucci, S. 141

Sapphire Technologies 129

Savvas, A. 133, 135

scalability of customer extranets 106

Scheepers, R. 9

Schneider, L. 141

Scottish Power 57

search and indexing in electronic DMS 66

search engines 29-31

security 122-30, 148

    BS 7799 standard 123-4

    Data Protection Act 118, 124-5

    in electronic document management systems 65

    of extranets 100, 112

    internet access control 126-8

    internet/intranet misuse 125-6

    needs, identifying 130

    Regulation of Investigatory Powers Bill 128-9

    in teleworking 102-3

    of workflow products 97

Selker, T. 145

server set-up costs 12

service providers 63

shared reference library 88

Sheppard, P.J. 90

Simple Mail Transfer Protocol (SMTP) 6, 7

simulation functions in WfMS 94

Skeldon, P. 137

Skinner, S. 105, 106

smart phones 133

software, and workflow products 95

'spam' 78

    rerouting 79-80

Stancich, L. 28

Stenmark, D. 30

STN 38

supplier extranet systems 109-11

    benefits 109-10

supply chain management (SCM) 109

SurfControl Plc 129

Swantek, K. 120

Sweet, P. 143

Tandy Corporation 69

task management in WfMS 94

Taylor, J. 139

TBC Research 108

TCA 104

TeamSite (Interwoven) 69

technical support of workflow products 96

The Telework, Telecottage and Telecentre Association 104

teleworking 101-4

   disadvantages 102

Telnet 7

Terdiman, R. 136

TMS Consulting 19

Trade and Industry, Department of 122, 124-5, 130

training

   in business applications 47-51

   costs 12-13

   groupware for 89-90

   on information overload 81-2

Transmission Control Protocol/Internet Protocol (TCP/IP) 6

transnational intranets/extranets 115-21

   case study 120-1

   interface, standardising 119-20

   language 115-18

   legal issues 118-19

Tung, L.L. 85

Turner, C. 128

ubiquitous computing 144-5

UK National Computing Centre 55

Ultimate BB 91

Ultra Board 91

UltraNet 41

unified messaging 137-40

Unipart 49

unsubscribe to services policy 80

The User Group 78

user interfaces in customer extranets 107-8

user needs in workflow products 96

Varnum, K. 45, 75

Vauxhall Motors 49

VDAB 81

vendor viability in customer extranet 108-9

vendor/product reputation in workflow products 95

Verity 33, 34

Verity Inc. 33

Virtual Private Networks (VPNs) 99-100, 112, 113, 136

Virtual University 48-9

'virus warning do-gooder' 78

voice over IP 107, 142-3

Vowler, J. 123

Vriens, D.J. 33, 84

Walder, B. 34

Walker, J. 51

Waltner, C. 68

Warren, L. 20

web browsers

    selective browsing 82

    standardisation 119

    success of 7-8

web content, enhancing 72-4

Web year 57-8

WebBoard 91

webflow interfaces in WfMS 94

webmaster 56, 59

Websense 126, 129

Weinberg, N. 145

Weiser, M. 144-5

Wendland, R. 135, 142

Whitlock, N.W. 68

Whittle, S. 125

Wielen, J. 104

wireless application protocol (WAP) 133, 135

wireless computing 132-5

Wireless Mark-up Language (WML) 135

Wirral Metropolitan College 33, 49

Wise, C. 27

Workflow Management Coalition 92, 97

workflow management systems (WfMS) 88, 91-8

workload analysis in WfMS 93

World Wide Web 6

Xerox 144

    case study 26-8

Yahoo! 141

Zetie, C. 133

Zimmerman, B. 50, 89